Dialogic Life

Charles Taylor and *The Ethics of Authenticity*

An Introduction and Guide

Stephen Loxton

Dialogic Life

Charles Taylor and *The Ethics of Authenticity*

An Introduction and Guide

Stephen Loxton
2022

Published by New Generation Publishing in 2022

First Edition

ISBN: 978-1-80369-980-6

www.newgeneration-publishing.com

New Generation Publishing

For Mark Felstead – a great colleague and a true friend.

Also by Stephen Loxton:

Plato and Aristotle (2013). Wells, Pushme Press.*
Religious Language (2013). Wells, Pushme Press.*
Conscience (2014). Wells, Pushme Press.*

Words and Deeds: An Introduction to the Thought of Ludwig Wittgenstein (Revised Second Edition 2020). London, New Generation Publishing.

Nietzsche and the Old Flame: An Introduction and Guide to Nietzsche *and On the Genealogy of Morals*. (2021) London, New Generation Publishing.

Forthcoming:

Proper Guardians: J S Mill's *On Liberty: an Introduction and Guide*.

*Updated and revised second editions of the books published by Pushme Press are being prepared for re-publication.

Photographs in this book are all courtesy of Shutterstock. The cover photograph is of Lake Moraine, in the Canadian Rockies.

Contents

Illustrations

Introduction

This book is offered as an introduction and guide to the thought of Charles Taylor (b. 1931) with particular reference to his work of 1991, *The Ethics of Authenticity*. Taylor's book is a set text within the International Baccalaureate's Philosophy course and is a text that may well be studied in the context of other courses at undergraduate level. This book is written for those who teach and those who study for any such course. However, it may well be interesting to readers wanting to learn about Taylor or looking for a way into modern philosophy.

The ideas for this book go back to the academic year 2013-14 when I took over an I.B Philosophy class. I knew that my predecessor had issued the class with *The Ethics of Authenticity* to read over the long holiday. When they returned, it seemed that none of them had made much of a start with the book. In any case, we began the term studying ethics, looking at metaethics and then normative and applied ethics. Then we turned to political philosophy. In the light of all this, we then began to read and discuss the Taylor, with the view that our studies of ethics and political philosophy should equip us well for the task.

Prior to this, in planning how to tackle the text, I realised that there was no published study guide available, so I wrote my own notes and linked power-points to aid my teaching and give my students some help in their reading and study. Here I followed my approach in preparing to teach other set books on this and similar courses. My usual method was to introduce the writer, discuss the key elements of their life and work, and then read and discuss the book in a series of classes until we had worked through the whole text. The students made notes from discussion and reading, and using past examination questions, they regularly wrote essays. This way, they built up their ideas on and responses to the text without too many other extraneous influences. Instead, they were fuelled by the discussions, questions, and provisional solutions reached through the exoteric medium of class discussion and review. At the end of each run through the text, I issued a version of my notes as a study guide and commentary to aid the students in their ongoing revision: the study guide was reviewed and updated over the years and eventually developed into this book.[1]

From this experience, my advice to those who will be using this guide to help in teaching Taylor's book is that the first thing to do is always to use a series of classes to read and discuss the sections that make up *The Ethics of Authenticity*. For example, within the I.B. Philosophy course, it is a valuable focus for study: It links well with the themes of ethics and political philosophy and is a compact read. Although it contains some idiosyncratic terminology, it is quite a straightforward text to work through with many ideas to review and discuss. When preparing to teach the text, it is a good idea to use discussion questions to aid attentive reading and to provoke ongoing discussion and revision. I have appended some of these that might be helpful to each of the commentary chapters below.

As we will see, *The Ethics of Authenticity* began life as a series of radio talks in Canada, and Taylor works hard to make his ideas clear. In the published form, the text is divided into ten sections – Taylor never calls them chapters – and in my experience, each of these can be read over and discussed in one or two one-hour lessons. In contrast to some set texts, it is relatively easy to plan a sequence of lessons to read and discuss each section and be fairly sure that you will be able to stick to it.

---

[1] In my book on Wittgenstein – Loxton (2020) – I wrote on Taylor in a chapter reviewing perspectives on ethics, prior to a chapter looking at Wittgenstein's approach to ethics. The material I drew on derived from my study guide to Taylor upon which this book is also based. Here some of the material used earlier is again in evidence, albeit in the context of a much fuller review of Taylor's whole position.

This book is organised as follows: after this Introduction, the first chapter gives an overview of Taylor's life and career, drawing largely on an autobiographical piece from 2008. The second chapter introduces *The Ethics of Authenticity* and explores the opening section of the text. Chapters 3 to 11 deal similarly with the remaining nine sections of the text. Chapter 12 considers some matters arising, and the final chapter offers conclusions on Taylor's enterprise.

In reviewing Taylor's ideas, the focus is on the main lines of explanation and analysis that he pursues. There is no attempt to give a line-by-line exegesis of the text: the method is to identify, illustrate and clarify the themes that are addressed; issues arising are identified as we go along, and the chapters are arranged in sub-sections with titles as a guide to the key matters that are under consideration; as mentioned, some key problems are revisited and discussed in the final two chapters.[1]

A final point to make at this stage concerns some conventions on understanding the relationship between morality and ethics. There are two contrasting lines of thought in the tradition of ethical writing: one takes the view that the terms 'moral' and 'ethical' are interchangeable.[2] On this view, there is no purpose in distinguishing the terms as in use, their meanings are more or less identical; both express and deal with our feelings and thoughts about what is 'good', bad', 'just', 'right', wrong', and so on. In contrast, it can be said that there is some value in sustaining a clear distinction between what we can term the 'moral' and the

---

[1] Footnotes are numbered afresh on each page and so all references or points made in this way will be at the foot of the page in question.

[2] This view is exemplified by Peter Singer who thinks there is no merit in making a distinction between 'moral' and 'ethical'. See Singer (2011) p. 1.

'ethical'.[1] The thought behind this is that the human condition invariably gives rise to concerns over what is 'right' or 'good' or 'just', and how it is that we behave and choose so as to act well and become of good character; these concerns and issues give life a *moral* texture. Moral problems can give rise to strong feelings and suggest that life has an ambiguous and challenging feel. In relation to life and the moral issues embroidering it, an *ethic* is a reasoned way, a method of consistently coping with, if not solving these moral issues, perhaps giving life a more secure feel.

Philosophical reflection on moral experience and ethical reasoning can lead to a metaethical audit of the terms in use to establish which can be used with cognitive confidence.[2] Developed ethical theories are usually termed *normative ethics*. Typical normative ethical theories might have the form and content of utilitarian consequentialism, classical or more modern variants of virtue theory, or the fusion of reason, autonomy, good will, and personhood in Kant's ethical project.[3]

This outline of procedural options within ethics is rehearsed for the simple reason that when readers come to *The Ethics of Authenticity,* it sounds very much as if Taylor will set out a normative ethic, giving a reasoned explanation and justification for a theory of deliberation and action over the moral tensions that arise in human life. As we shall soon discover, Taylor does not operate in the conventional style of most moral philosophers. He eschews the metaethical audit, and what he does in his text does not produce a normative ethic of the usual kind.

---

[1] This approach is exemplified by Lawrence Hatab – see Hatab (2000) pp 2-4.
[2] See Moore (1965) for an example of this.
[3] See Foot (2003) for an example of this within the modern tradition of virtue ethics.

16

These points provide some operational guidelines to keep in mind as we examine Taylor's work, seeing as we proceed what he does and why he does it, particularly as we sift his ideas, assessing what we have in terms of form and content with the 'ethic of authenticity'.

Stephen Loxton

McGill University in Montreal – the Faculty of Arts Building. Charles Taylor read History at McGill (1949-1952). He returned to lecture in 1961 and was later Professor of Philosophy and Political Science. He is now Professor Emeritus.

Balliol College, Oxford. Charles Taylor won a Rhodes Scholarship and was an Undergraduate and then Postgraduate student at Balliol (1952-56). He read Politics, Philosophy and Economics at Oxford, graduating in 1955. After a year of postgraduate study, Taylor gained a Prize Fellowship at All Souls College.

1. Charles Taylor – a Philosophical Life

Charles Taylor is a Canadian philosopher whose reputation was largely made through his publications on Hegel in the 1970s and from two later studies, *Sources of the Self* (1989)[1] – a book Taylor draws on mightily in *The Ethics of Authenticity*[2] – and A *Secular Age* (2007). Taylor's work has won several accolades, and he continues to lecture and write on the themes in which he has an interest.[3]

As a thinker bringing historical concerns to bear in examining ethical and political strands of philosophy, Taylor considers that humans have distinct qualities and capacities as individuals while also being social creatures who live, learn, think, and operate in communities. He thinks it is clear that political and moral life is framed and considered in communal terms against the historical and cultural backdrop to the social institutions of the present.

Taylor is also keen to promote the individual's capacity for a mode of life characterised by self-critical reflection. He values qualities and potentialities while promoting individuality; however, he also opposes trends identified in modernity that manifest over self-orientated forms of individualism.

It is a matter of emphasis, but Taylor's outlook contrasts with the more radical liberal theories in politics and ethics in which the sovereign individual is presented as the focus

---

[1] Hereafter *Sources* will often be used as the abbreviation for *Sources of the Self*.
[2] Hereafter *Authenticity* will often used for *The Ethics of Authenticity*.
[3] Taylor's awards include: Companion of the Order of Canada (1996); The Templeton Prize (2007); The Kyoto Prize (2008); The John W. Kluge Prize (2015); The Berggruen Prize (2016). The prizes here are given for work that significantly advances understanding of humane, scientific, cultural, and spiritual matters.

for ethical and political discussion.[1]

Charles Taylor's life and interest in philosophy are given a useful presentation in a lecture he gave in 2008. This is the Kyoto Prize Commemorative Lecture, entitled 'What drove me to philosophy?'[2] He explains that as a boy, he had the typically philosophical sense of wonderment about reality, along the lines of the classic metaphysical question of 'why there is something instead of nothing?' Perhaps it is not so uncommon a feature of youthful human activity to reflect on these matters. The less common thing is to keep the wonderment going, which is what Taylor certainly did. He explains that he became engaged with the sense of 'puzzlement' about resolving fundamental questions. This is an oscillating theme through Taylor's writing, and it was the sense of puzzlement that led Taylor to philosophy.

Philosophy, says Taylor, 'is all about articulating what has never been properly said', and the key point is that it is not just philosophy that engages with this. Other areas of expression have deep relevance: 'poetry, music, art, can all struggle with the same deep intuitions'. Philosophy, of course, 'has its own medium', and in the lecture, Taylor says he was 'being propelled towards it' from a young age. However, the wide spectrum of concern had some impact, for Taylor was initially propelled to university to study history.

Taylor attended McGill University in Montreal, graduating in 1952. He explains that history gave him the chance to study human life and, through providing a framework,

---

[1] J. S. Mill's *On Liberty* of 1859 is the classic statement of this view. See Mill (1987).
[2] The lecture is available online: The 2008 Kyoto Prize Commemorative Lecture https://www.kyotoprize.org/wp/wp-content/uploads/2016/02/24kC_lct_EN.pdf. Quotations in this chapter are all from this lecture unless otherwise indicated. All online sources are as cited in the relevant footnote.

relate this to his interests in how 'politics can transform human life'. At a deeper level, he also realised that his growing interest was in what he calls 'philosophical anthropology', that is, a philosophical view of humanity and human development. This was a larger topic than those usually dealt with within history and politics, and as often considered, they present, says Taylor, as giving a 'stripped-down, reductive view of human life.' Taylor clarifies that a large focus in his subsequent work has been to 'combat this kind of reductive, over simple, one-dimensional understanding'. This links with Taylor's interest in how humans could 'transform themselves' by their endeavours of thought and action, which led to a commitment to activism in politics that went beyond theoretical study.

Montreal: a view over the Saint Lawrence River towards the city of Montreal, Charles Taylor's home town.

Although political activism often engaged his interest, Taylor continued his studies. His work at McGill had gone well, and his intellectual interests were growing. He won a Rhodes Scholarship to study at Oxford and was a student of Balliol College. He read for a degree in Politics, Philosophy and Economics, graduating in 1955.

At Oxford, Taylor found that smooth and contented work was less straightforward: he found the mainstream work in Oxford's approach to philosophy to be arid and worryingly anti-historical.

As he explains:

'My first real encounter with academic philosophy was at Oxford; and I was appalled with what I saw as a dry, positivistic style, which seemed to devalue and dismiss the deepest, most important questions of life. What is more, I became aware of how a similar spirit was dominant in the sciences of human life, in psychology and political science for instance. Further study in this climate seemed to offer only frustration and discouragement'.

Taylor's problem was that of the gulf he sensed between real, active, engaged, historically conscious human life on the one hand and Oxford's philosophy on the other, which at the time, had a preoccupation with what was termed linguistic or ordinary-language philosophy. This approach tended to make philosophy a second-order discipline of study: life and the issues arising were not the focus. Instead, philosophers worked to perfect techniques of analysis, auditing linguistic usage and proposing some legitimate and rejecting many allegedly illegitimate expressive forms. Typically, natural science might be granted more validity for its culture of thought and its modes of enquiry than history, literary criticism, or the philosophy of human anthropology.

Taylor found these trends reductive and artificial. His historically informed preference for philosophical anthropology fuelled a crucial reaction. Writing about this in an earlier piece, he notes that 'the world of analytic philosophy' and 'Anglo-Saxon moral philosophy' were prone to a form of 'narrowness' in terms of both the 'range of doctrines considered' and 'the range of questions that it seems sensible to ask.'[1] The upshot was that this tradition tended to see morality as centred on 'questions of what we ought to do', neglecting questions that focussed on 'what it is good to be and what it is good to love.'

---

[1] Taylor: 'Iris Murdoch and Moral Philosophy', in Antonaccio and Schweiker (1996) p. 3.

These are deeply salient remarks, for Taylor centres much of what he goes on to write on providing an alternative to the conventional tradition in modern moral philosophy. The alternative line is cultivated in his ongoing career and comes to expression in works such as *Sources* and *Authenticity*. What we get is the idea that life, human life, both the life of individuals and humans in association, is a whole package. What we are and what we do as humans, through our endeavours, creativity, and relationships, is seen as something complex but something to be understood as a whole.

This means that Taylor does not favour readings of the human condition that entail a prioritisation of something – pure reason, for example, or alternatively, feelings – over the rest. It also means that Taylor is inclined to work with reference to the individual human condition as much more embedded in communal, social, historical and cultural realities. As we shall see, this gives life a highly interpersonal and a residually moral character. It also shows that it matters that human life is embedded in the wider culture.

A stimulus for Taylor's outlook and a means to cultivate the insights so as to construct an alternative came from his reading into modern European thought, particularly the French phenomenologist Maurice Merleau-Ponty.[1] Here he found what he regarded as a tradition with a richer focus on the philosophy of life, where the issues of what it means to be human and what it is to live a good life had real currency and orientation to an ethical concern for the world in general.

Taylor also found some positive influences within the milieu of Oxford philosophy. He was positively influenced by the work and ideas of the philosopher and novelist Iris

---

[1] Maurice Merleau-Ponty (1908-1961).

Murdoch, whose interests in ethics and moral philosophy focused on the moral character that the individual developed through attentive relationships and the value of living towards the ideal of the Good, which she understood in moderated Platonic terms.[1] Taylor retained a high regard for her thinking, and in his later work, the sense of a 'moral ontology' he expresses is derived in part from Murdoch.[2]

Given his objections to what might be termed over-theoretical approaches in philosophy and his interest in activism, it is no surprise that Taylor embroidered his years of study with periods when he engaged more practically in political matters. While at Oxford, he became the students' President of the Campaign for Nuclear Disarmament. In 1956, with the advent of the Hungarian uprising, Taylor left off his ongoing studies and went to help in a refugee centre in Vienna. Later, in the 1960s, this more practical urge resurfaced, and he campaigned in Canadian elections for the New Democratic Party, standing for election, albeit unsuccessfully. He also worked with other commissions and reforming agencies in Canada, his view being that the work of teaching philosophy was always enhanced by the business of dealing with people within political society and working on their concerns, interests and the issues of the day. His interests involved looking to promote the sense in which, as he puts it in the Kyoto Lecture, 'mutual trust and a sense of common political identity' can be strengthened, this in settings that are invariably multicultural. To promote wider inclusion in the political state, he also engaged with a style of political education to develop 'a common understanding of democratic citizenship'.

Despite these commitments to practical political matters, Taylor' studies went well, and he moved on to postgraduate work while still at Balliol. Then in 1956, he won a Prize Fellowship at All Souls College and decamped there.

---

[1] See Murdoch (1970) and (1992). Dame Isis Murdoch (1919-1999).
[2] See *Sources* p. 8. We comment more on this 'moral ontology' below.

Through the later 1950s, he was researching for a doctorate, drawing on his wider reading of continental thinkers. Taylor was still looking to develop and articulate views that challenged what he saw as the restricted outlook favoured by the Oxford philosophers. He was awarded his doctorate in 1961, having been supervised by Sir Isaiah Berlin, then the most eminent specialist historian of ideas.[1]

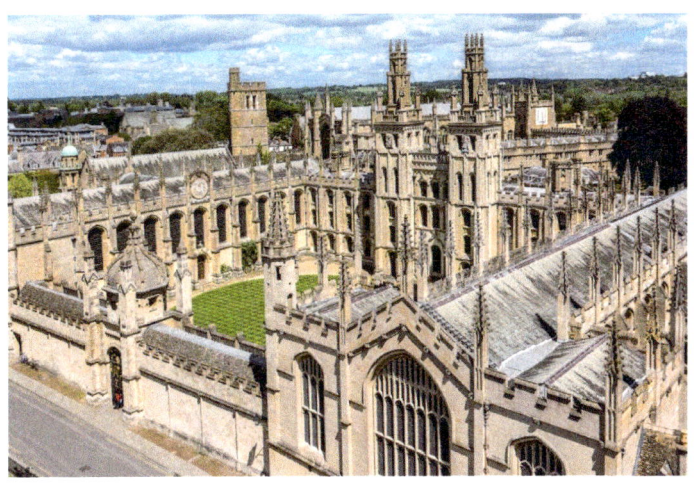

All Souls College, Oxford. Charles Taylor was a Prize Fellow here as a Postgraduate studying for his doctorate (1956-61). He returned to the College as a Fellow and as Chichele Professor of Social and Political Theory at the University of Oxford (1976-1981). He then became a Quandom Fellow of the College.

In terms of Taylor's thinking, the philosophical anthropology he developed is an outcome of what he calls 'a hybrid training'. He means that his ongoing work is 'philosophical to the extent that it takes a stand on certain fundamental issues in anthropology, and social-scientific to the extent that it gathers and tries to explain data about society and history'.

---

[1] Sir Isaiah Berlin (1909-1997). Berlin was a Fellow of All Souls and later became the founding President of Wolfson College in 1965.

As noted earlier, Taylor's thinking takes seriously the point that humans are not to be seen simply as individual reasoning agents, nor are they simply creatures of instinct and feeling. Humans are reasoning agents, and the human capacity for reasoning is something Taylor always wants to promote. However, he also wants to retain the more complex sense mentioned earlier as to what it is to be human, the view that the human condition is to be considered as one where individuals and individualised thinkers develop their lives and so their values through living within a textured backdrop, in a context, a setting, a community, language and culture. They are nurtured in their understanding and development with regard to thoughts and feelings in a fusion with others in a background of shared meaning and value, and this process provides the means by which individuals make sense of each other and themselves.

An indication of the focus for Taylor's thinking comes from the title of his first book. Based on his doctoral thesis, *The Explanation of Behaviour* (1964) examines a range of behaviourist theories of human conduct, which are attacked for having too narrow a view through being centred on the immediate conditioning circumstances alleged to make us what we turn out to be. Against this, Taylor argued for the richer, more varied patterns of influence that empower us, along with our capacity for reason, to be capable of becoming what we choose to be. In his subsequent thought, this theme is often to the fore: what we turn out to be in the scenarios of our life is never the favoured theme. What counts is what we choose to be, in relation to others and our collective tradition. Taylor is not, we might note, troubled by thoughts of rigid determinism.

In this work and his ongoing career, Taylor is consistent in attacking 'reductive explanations' and defending his preferred sense of 'philosophical anthropology'. This is, he says, 'a philosophical account of human nature or the human condition. This would ideally reflect the wonder at the greatness but at the same time strangeness of human life'. In giving a profile of the character of the human condition, Taylor is elaborating a version of something else we mentioned earlier, what he refers to as a 'moral ontology'.[1] He means that to be a critically reflective individual, living in relation to others in the world of common experience gives rise to the realisation that life, or being, is impregnated with evaluative activity. Choices, commitments and preferences all signal values as being embedded in the process and procedures of being human. Taylor has the thought that in modernity, this moral ontology has been suppressed, in part by some reactions to 'the pluralist nature of modern society' as well as by the predominance of 'modern epistemology'.[2]

More confirmation of the character of the moral ontology that Taylor develops comes through the business of giving a 'philosophical account' of two distinct things that he runs together: 'human nature' and 'the human condition'. In expressing the point, Taylor says that he wants to characterise his 'philosophical anthropology' as 'a philosophical account of human nature or the human condition'. By conjoining these issues with the powerful term 'or', Taylor might mean that he will argue that questions of human nature and the human condition are to be run together, or that they are distinct, or are variations on one theme. Tactically, the 'or' in Taylor's sentence is best not seen as denoting a relation of equivalence, since it is one thing to set out within a 'philosophical anthropology' a view of 'human nature'; it is another to explore the 'human condition': one study is likely to focus on what humans are, and the other on how humans live. It might be that we decide, in our study, that humans are best understood through insights into how they live and that the two matters run together. However, it is as well not assuming that at the start.

---

[1] See *Sources* pp. 3-24.
[2] *Sources* p. 10.

As we move on, and indeed in his work in general, there is no doubt that what Taylor has in mind is that it is a consistent feature that humans are troubled by the issue of what it means to be. What Taylor thinks and appeals to is, as noted earlier, the notion that *all* of us are troubled in this way. We could say that as far as Taylor is concerned, it is in the nature of being authentically human to be concerned about the wider human condition. It is through this perspective on the human condition that Taylor does not favour setting theories of life, or morality, apart from life. He sees this as always reductive and as a mistake. Instead, he wants to develop insights woven from the tapestry of life, centring his philosophical outlook on the strands of thought that he found in the continental tradition, which ties in with one of the things that philosophy of the type he preferred should do. As he puts it in the Kyoto Lecture, philosophy in this style helps to 'reduce the perplexity' of life, and it does this by minimising the 'bad, reductive views of the human being' and trying to replace these 'with a coherent view which resolves the puzzles which we all experience about our own existence'.

Even though Taylor considers that he has not progressed far in finding resolutions, the 'force of perplexity is still driving me on'. Here, we should note that Taylor's remarks are testimony to his assumption that we humans have 'puzzles… we all experience about our own existence'. The 'all' here is a significant point, and to explore the specifics here, we need to make a brief detour into the history of thought – something we often do in dealing with Taylor.

It is fair to say that perplexity and puzzlement are characteristic terms for Taylor to use to convey his sense that philosophy is a reaction to how we – we all, he means – 'wonder at the world'. What is definite in his orientation of how to respond to this sense of life and reality being problematic is that it is partly due to his reaction against some aspect of the mainstream of early-modern philosophy that would have been influential in the philosophical styles he encountered at Oxford. Taylor sees the origins of mechanical and reductive thinking in philosophy in the tradition that can be seen as emerging from aspects of the work and influence of Thomas Hobbes and René Descartes.[1]

Descartes (a rationalist) and Hobbes (a materialist) are two thinkers who sit at the start of the period of modernity. They also present quite distinctly, with some clear and spectacular differences. Prefiguring the theme of a later song by Madonna, both take the view that the body is a part of the material world. Hobbes took what we term the mind in much the same way. Descartes considered the mind to be quite distinct from the matter from which the body and the rest of reality were composed.[2]

Taylor will have something more to say about this, but at this point, what we must stress is that he thinks that these orientations are all artificial and misleading. He considers that the later materialism of Karl Marx was as distorting, with its view that the socio-economic processes of production were determinative of thought and ideas.[3]

Taylor's view is that all of these approaches devalue human life and do so because throughout the whole sweep of the last four hundred years, scientific thinking takes a predominant hold. Taylor's view is that this influence has been reductive.

---

[1] Thomas Hobbes (1588-1679): René Descartes (1596-1650). The two were acquainted.

[2] One difference between Hobbes and Descartes is, as indicated briefly in the text, over their contrasting estimates of reality. Hobbes favours a materialist view, a kind of monism, thinking all of reality is composed of one sort of stuff, variously arranged. Descartes thinks the material world is like this, but that what we might term mind, soul, thought, and self-consciousness, were of another mental substance. Descartes thus has a form of substance dualism.

[3] Karl Marx (1818-1883).

Taylor returned to Canada in 1961 to teach at McGill. Over the next decades, this was one main base for his life and work. He became Professor of Philosophy and Political Science, and in due course, Professor Emeritus. He also spent time at Oxford, becoming Chichele Professor of Social and Political Thought and a Fellow of All Souls.[1] Arising from his lecturing career, his reputation was strengthened by, as mentioned, two studies of Hegel, published in 1975 and 1979.[2] He then developed the ideas that eventually came to bear in his major work, *Sources of the Self* (1989).

In *Sources*, Taylor drew on a wide range of literary and philosophical traditions and styles to elaborate and explain the development of human identity or selfhood, where selfhood was particularly understood to reach a high point as the dispassionate, rational individual. He saw this as involving 'a new understanding of human agency and its characteristic powers'.[3] This view brings 'new conceptions of the good and new locations of moral sources: an ideal of self-responsibility, with the new definitions of freedom and reason accompanying it, and the connected sense of dignity.'

Taylor's idea is that this outlook has become the condition of how we think and live, so that 'we see this way as being normal, as anchored in perennial human nature in the way our physical organs are. So we come to think we "have" selves as we have heads.' Taylor is keen to iron home that the thinking here, giving the definition of human agency in terms of 'the self', is a consequence of a 'linguistic

---

[1] In this role at Oxford he succeed Sir Isaiah Berlin, who held the Chichele Professorship 1965-1976.
[2] See Taylor (1975) and (1979). G.W.F. Hegel (1770-1831): a leading figure in German philosophy in the romantic era, his reputation being made with the publication of *Phenomenology of Spirit* (1807).
[3] *Sources* p. 177.

reflection of our modern understanding'. The perspective that is suggested has a radical aspect in putting the focus on what it is to be human on a form of inwardness, giving rise to a modern culture that is individualist in character. Taylor portrays this modernity as follows:

'… it prizes autonomy; it gives an important place to self-exploration, in particular of feeling; and its visions of the good life generally involve personal commitment. As a consequence, in its political language, it formulates the immunities due people in terms of subjectivist rights. Because of its egalitarian bent, it conceives these rights as universal.'[1]

In *Sources*, Taylor does a good deal to suggest that this was, in fact, a reductive rather than positive model for humanity. A tension arises in Taylor's analysis since modernity is commonly fond of defending variant forms of personal or individual rights. In contrast, Taylor often casts 'rights', particularly 'subjectivist rights', in qualitatively negative terms, and for some readers, this presents as one of the more challenging moves we find him making.[2]

In *Sources*, Taylor undertakes a considerable mission to recover the 'constitutive goods' as he calls them, that serve as the real moral sources for human identity, even in modernity.[3] We consider Taylor's thinking on this later in our study.

In due course, the problems and a sketch of the solutions that Taylor had in mind came to a more popular expression when he was invited to deliver the 1991 Massey Lectures to be aired by Canadian Broadcasting Service Radio.

---

[1] *Sources* p. 305.
[2] Taylor is more amenable to positive rights, that it, rights that are established in statute law. See *Authenticity* p. 114. On how positive liberty can become dictatorial, see Berlin (2017) pp. 193-200.
[3] Sources p. 92. See also pp. 495 and 498.

The University of Toronto. Charles Taylor delivered the Massey Lectures in 1991 on 'The Malaise of Modernity'. The Massey Lectures are considered Canada's most prominent public lecture series and emanate from Massey College, a part of the University of Toronto. They started in 1961 as a tribute to the College's founder, Vincent Massey (1887-1967), a former Governor-General of Canada.[1]

The Massey Lectures were a part of the 'Ideas' series that the radio station was running. Taylor entitled his lectures 'The Malaise of Modernity'. There were five lectures in the broadcast series, and then, in an expanded form, Taylor published the lectures as a book, unsurprisingly called *The Malaise of Modernity*. The text was published in Canada under this title, but later in the year, the identical text was republished in the USA with the title *The Ethics of Authenticity*, and this is the version that has become best known.

Taylor's thinking up to this point, and indeed in his subsequent work, shows enthusiasm for several key themes that we can note from what he says in 'What drove me to philosophy?' One is the necessity of 'a plurality of solutions' to problem-solving for social and cultural life. Taylor explains that his insights against what we can term

[1] Details can found on the College's website at https://www.masseycollege.ca/programs-and-events/programs/cbc-massey-lectures/

single-shot solutions came from his upbringing in a bilingual Anglo-French home. From this, he got a sense of how 'two languages can reflect the world very differently'. Taylor takes from this bilingual upbringing an insight for his ongoing work that human perceptions, feelings, thoughts and behaviours are all bound up with the expressive and reflective business of language use, where that usage stems from social, cultural and historical settings.

An issue lurking here is how diversity and equality of interest within a pluralism sit with the subjectivism and relativism that might be thought to tie in with these themes. Are we not here embracing all of these as aspects of a plural modernity?

Taylor is eager to explore the historical means by which we come to this state of affairs. One of his larger thoughts is to be alert to and sceptical about what he terms 'the dominant master narrative of Western modernity'. This is the theme arising in the Enlightenment, that 'the human race goes through a number of stages, defined by the manner in which humans make their living; hunter-gatherers give way to nomads who are in turn succeeded and overwhelmed by agricultural societies. These last are finally succeeded by "commercial" societies'. To this sequence, we can add the 'industrial', 'post-industrial' and 'electronic' stages – and we might now add the refinement of the '.com' stage. What Taylor sees as wrong in this view is the assumption that human development follows a distinct and irreversible series of moves that also leads to enhanced, law-abiding civilization. Here we might think that Taylor, the student of, and teacher on Hegel, inclines to be more of a 'left' than a 'right' Hegelian.[1] He is also an astute enough reader of the trends of human history and culture to see that humanity can experience declines as well as rises in civilisation and that

---

[1] Hegel's followers were classified as either 'right' (or 'old') or 'left' (or 'young') Hegelians, meaning conservative or radical in how respectively they interpreted and applied Hegelian thought.

nothing is more certain to bring about cultural decline than ideological overconfidence in the singularity of a given cultures' self-esteem.

What Taylor likes, and is fond of referencing in his writing in general, are views that suggest the fluidity and impermanence as an aspect of the individual human condition coupled to a focus on the securities for the life of the individual within a social context. He likes to locate and develop a sense of how a balanced and inclusive outlook on life can be achieved, and in this, the work of Montaigne is especially relevant.[1]

In his *Essays*, and from the twenty years or more of reflection and writing that went into them, Montaigne found that instead of his reflectiveness giving a stronger and clearer sense of his mind, it exposed how thought, and the mind that engaged in thinking, 'bolted off like a runaway horse, taking far more trouble over itself than it ever did over anyone else; it gives birth to many chimeras and fantastic monstrosities, one after another, without order or fitness, that, so as to contemplate at my ease their oddness and their strangeness, I began to keep a record of them'.[2]

Amongst the insights these records of reflection provide, we have the following observation:

'In truth we are but nothing.'[3]

What Montaigne perceived was that our nothingness is a

---

[1] Michel De Montaigne (1533-1592). French aristocrat, soldier, classicist, landowner and writer. Notable author of the *Essays* – see Montaigne (2003) – which is used for the passages from Montaigne cited here.
[2] Montaigne (2003) I. 8: p. 31. See *Sources* pp. 178-184 where Taylor discusses Montaigne. Taylor quotes Montaigne from a French edition – see *Sources* p. 544.
[3] Montaigne (2003) II. 12: p. 55

qualitative state of limitation, which follows from the fact that:

'… each part of us is less than the whole: we are part of the world: the world is, therefore, provided with wisdom and reason more abundantly than we are.'[1]

With this, we have a classic instance of the kind of insight that Taylor prizes, and akin to what he will defend in what he wants to promote in *Authenticity*. Montaigne's point is that if humans fail to appreciate their state of limitation, not seeing that the true human condition is being a part of a greater whole, then the danger is that human lives are set on the quest for definite individual truths and values, and this leads us to give 'free reign' to our opinions.[2] We prop ourselves up with our own 'ingenuity', and so deceive ourselves.

Montaigne's thought is that the human soul, cast in feminine guise, 'can never find a sure footing':

'… she is too confused and weak for that. She roams about seeking bases for her hopes and consolations in conditions which are foreign to her nature. She clings to them and puts down roots. These notions which she ingeniously forges for herself may be ever so frivolous and fantastic, but she can find repose in them more surely than in herself, and much more willingly.'

Taylor is especially happy with another line of thought from Montaigne:

'… there is no permanent existence in our being or in that of objects. We ourselves, our faculty of judgement and all mortal things are flowing and rolling ceaselessly: nothing certain can be established about one from another, since both judged and judging are ever shifting and changing… We have no communication with Being; as human nature is wholly situated, for ever, between birth

---

[1] Montaigne (2003) II. 12: p. 594.
[2] Montaigne (2003) II. 12: p. 622.

and death, it shows itself on as a dark, shadowy appearance, an unstable, weak opinion. And if you should determine to try and grasp what Man's *being* is, it would be exactly like trying to hold a fistful of water: the more tightly you squeeze anything the nature of which is to flow, the more you will lose what you try to retain in your grasp.'[1]

Taylor endorses Montaigne's very clear sense that rather than base an outlook on 'the exemplary, the universal, or the edifying', it was better to observe what could be found from studying the 'the contours of the changing reality of one being, himself'.[2] This Taylor links to Montagne's notable insight that the 'whole of moral philosophy' can be attached to 'a commonplace private life just as well as to one of richer stuff.'[3] Montagne thinks this as he considers that 'every man bears the whole Form of the human condition.'[4] What Montaigne meant with this affirmation about 'every man' was that what every person experienced and could therefore give some account of was what it was to be human – so the more we associate with others, the better we would understand 'the human condition' in which we also participated.

Taylor is keen to endorse the balanced approach that comes through Montaigne's self-reflection, the avoidance of extremes and ultimate ideals, and our self-acceptance of limitation. In promoting the importance of accepting 'what we are', Montaigne thus provides an inauguration 'of one of the recurring themes of modern culture.'[5]

---

[1] Montaigne (2003) II. 12: p. 680. Taylor cites this passage – *Sources* pp. 178-179.

[2] *Sources* p. 179.

[3] Montaigne (2003): III. 2: p. 908 – quoted by Taylor – see *Sources* p. 179.

[4] This insight has been influential in modern moral philosophy, as in the resurgent virtue ethics of Philippa Foot. See Foot (2003).

[5] *Sources* p. 181.

In his own work, as in the Kyoto Lecture, Taylor elaborates both an interest in 'diversity' and the sense of 'the harmonious co-existence of different groups'. He expresses this through the notion of 'multiple modernities', an idea that aims to testify to the notion of pluralistic and diverse social and cultural states we mentioned earlier. His sense is that in modernity, a range and variety of modern ideals of what it is to be human co-exist.[1] This implies a fusion of pluralism with a mode of relativism, linked with a capacity we have to abstract over and above the realm of particulars and relations so as to be cognisant of them.

In his approach, coupling historical study with the commitment to 'philosophical anthropology', Taylor works with a form of perspectivism to achieve the insights that allow the view that there is no one single line of explanatory development for how 'modernity' will come to bear 'in different societies and cultures'. Again, Taylor's appeal to a form of 'moral ontology' in *Sources* has a bearing on this, for his idea is that 'respect for life and integrity' are related to the widely regarded if variably expressed point that humans are generically 'rational agents and thus have a dignity which transcends any other being'.[2]

This line of thought leads to the sense that 'a moral reaction is an assent to, an affirmation of, a given ontology of the human.' Taylor affirms that humans possess deeper and more elemental 'moral instincts', to do with 'our ineradicable sense that human life is to be respected.'[3] The idea here is that this 'ineradicable sense' provides the operational 'mode of access to the world in which ontological claims are discernible and can be rationally argued about and sifted.'

With these comments, Taylor unwittingly provides

---

[1] See *Sources* Chapters 24 and 25.

[2] *Sources* p. 5.

[3] *Sources* p. 8.

operational imperatives that come to bear in *Authenticity*. The notion that 'human life is to be respected' is something that is implicit in a great deal of Taylor's thinking in *Authenticity*. The other term that is of the greatest significance is 'ontology', about which we need to say something more. Taylor is using this concept in the way common in continental thought, and it is associated particularly with the work of the phenomenological and existential philosopher Martin Heidegger.[1] As we will see, Heidegger's thinking anticipates and influences some of the themes we find in Taylor, so it is worth another digression.

In the review made in *Being and Time* (1927), Heidegger characterises the human condition as being marked out by what he calls the *ontological* question, in particular, noting the perplexity of '*the question of the meaning of our being.*'[2]

In his exploration, which in some respects harks back to the reflections of Montaigne, Heidegger employs the term 'Dasien' to denote the sense of what it is to live with the consciousness of one's life being placed within the wider setting of the human condition.[3] Humans have the unique capacity to be aware of and concerned about the meaning and purpose of their existence. Dasien, Heidegger remarks, 'is an entity... ontologically distinguished by the fact that, in its very Being, that Being is an *issue* for it.'[4]

Humans are seen as individuals living with the ambiguous sense that the meaning of our very existence is problematic. This sits with us as we go about the business of life, operating in the world, amongst others in everyday existence. Despite our living in the hurly-burly of social life, where we can be shaped and directed by others into all kinds

---

[1] Martin Heidegger (1889-1976).
[2] See Heidegger (2001) p. 20.
[3] Heidegger (2001) p. 26.
[4] Heidegger (2001) p. 32.

of roles that validate our social existence, we have the question of the meaning of our individual being bubbling away in the background. This, the ontological question, is, for Heidegger, the fundamental question for the human condition.

Heidegger also takes the view that in the history of Western thought, since Descartes' time – here anticipating some of Taylor's reservations about the French philosopher – the emphasis in philosophy on epistemology, on the problems of knowledge and certainty, has been too extreme, in somehow detaching thinking from being. Heidegger judges that issues of epistemology have a derivative and secondary significance, and that the emphasis on such issues serves only to cloud the primary area of concern.

Accordingly, again anticipating Taylor's concerns, Heidegger moves against aspects of the Cartesian tradition, with its concentration on mind, reason, and on consciousness as the basis for certainty, reflection and understanding. In Heidegger's work, there is a greater focus on the dynamic, social nature of being as the context for consciousness and an emphasis on the sense of anxiety that arises in the consciousness of this as the mode of being human.

From this, the central theme in *Being and Time* becomes a concern with ontological questions about being. Heidegger makes clear his appreciation of the extent to which modern philosophy has had a problem with reality – the problem of the relation between the 'in me' and the 'outside of me', as he puts it.[1]

Heidegger has in mind the various arguments and proofs that epistemology has attempted to show that we, as subjects, can understand the means and the extent to which

---

[1] Heidegger (2001) p. 248.

we can say that we know the object, reality. These epistemological considerations are seen as the 'scandal of philosophy', not meaning that it is scandalous that the problems have yet to be solved, but that it is scandalous that *'such proofs are expected and are attempted again and again.'* [1]

Heidegger's view is that such epistemological projects are problematic: they come, he says:

'… from an ontologically inadequate way of starting with *something* of such a character that independently *of it* and "outside" *of it* a "world" is to be proved as present-at-hand. It is not that the proofs are inadequate, but that the kind of Being of the entity which does the proving and makes requests for proofs has *not been made definite enough…* If Dasien is understood correctly, it defies such proofs, because in its Being it already *is* what subsequent proofs deem necessary to demonstrate for it.'

Heidegger's idea is that human self-awareness comes into consciousness as we become alert to and concerned about living as 'beings-in-the-world'. We are in a context, a setting, and a domain of possibilities within and as the socio-cultural world of our own life-history, where we live, act and choose amongst the others. It can be seen just from this how he then reasons that what we can do in a properly orientated epistemological quest is to determine *how* things are 'in-the-world'. Elemental questions about the meaning of life aside, even such questions as 'Why is my cat hungry?', 'Why does my daughter need a larger allowance?', and 'When will I finish this work, and will the sun then be shining?', resonate with meaning because we are each already existing in the mode of 'being-in-the-world'. This state of being provides the preconditions for the other sorts of specialist questions preoccupying the philosophers disapproved of by both Heidegger and Taylor.

---

[1] Heidegger (2001) p. 249.

Returning to Taylor's thinking about the pluralism in modern social life, the notion of 'multiple modernities' he uses is further explained in his book *Modern Social Imaginaries*.[1] He suggests that a core problem in the modern social sciences is:

'... modernity itself: that historically unprecedented amalgam of new practices and institutional forms (science, technology, industrial production, urbanization), of new ways of living (individualism, secularization, instrumental rationality), and of new forms of malaise (alienation, meaninglessness), a sense of impending social dislocation'.

It might make sense to call this simply the plurality of modernity, but Taylor does not do this. Instead, he poses the question of whether it makes sense to speak of 'a single phenomenon' of modernity or, as he thinks, to consider 'multiple modernities'. He favours the latter (plural) option. Modernity, as Taylor presents it, comes about in varied ways. To return to his core example, non-Western cultures 'cannot properly be understood if we try to grasp them in a general theory that was designed originally with the Western case in mind'.

Within this dominant narrative, Taylor sees that human life moves to be naturalistic and secular, with traditional religion falling into decline. Taylor does not wholly buy into this storyline, and he explores the issues arising in 'Living in a Secular Age', the Gifford Lectures delivered at Edinburgh University in 1999. The lectures were then expanded into *A Secular Age*.

In the Kyoto Lecture, Taylor says that in *A Secular Age,* he made a critique of 'the Grand Narrative of Secularization' as it applies in the West. He means that in Western societies, the history and development are 'much more diverse than was supposed, and the site of cross-currents undreamt of by

---

[1] Taylor (2004): quotations here are from the 'Introduction' pp. 1-2.

mainstream secularization theory'. In this matter, Taylor is again showing that some explanations are simplistic and too totalistic: the real situation is exposed as being a complex and multi-layered process, with the puzzles and perplexities once more coming into the foreground.

In *A Secular Age* and other writings, Taylor explores 'the place of the spiritual in human life'. Here he compliments a theme richly explored in the twentieth-century tradition of religious studies, of seeing human life as inextricably bound up with a spiritual dimension of experience that is more vital and more elemental than this, that or any particular religion.[1]

Linked to this, in the Lecture, Taylor moves on to explain that he is 'a person of faith', a Roman Catholic. He minimises the absolutism that might be thought of as inevitable with this allegiance, taking the view that in all religious and philosophical traditions, 'something important about the human condition is disclosed'. This boils down to the generalisation that something important in the sense of instructive can be gleaned from whatever it is that people are committed to in terms of their overarching beliefs, outlooks or ideologies. As a statement of intellectual policy, this is something of a truism, but it is another matter to agree on whether particular traditions are good, worthwhile or commendable, and another to assume that somehow they will be consistent.

Taylor seems mindful of this, as he employs some neo-theological terminology in referencing the 'demonic potentiality' that is closely allied to the spiritual dimension of human experience. He is consistent in thinking that we need to fuse an openness to study and review ideas and practices from other traditions, histories and cultures than our own and be prepared to consider the better and worse

---

[1] See for example, Otto (1958); Eliade (1959); Buber (2000); Cantwell-Smith (1978); Smart (1971); Macquarrie (1982).

aspects of human life that we find on both sides of the matter. Taylor's deeper and very important point is that the human desire for security and certitude of belief and outlook can lead to deviant forms of 'appalling hatred and destruction'. Religious and secular belief and value systems can be hardened into competing essentialisms that find greater strength and purity by 'projecting all evil onto the Other'.

In an article written for *The Guardian* in 2007, Taylor characterised the problem here as 'block thinking':

'Block thinking fuses a varied reality into one indissoluble unity.'[1]

By this, he means the form of generalised absolutism that, post 9/11, led some in the western world to see the 'same core meaning' expressed in the many and varied forms of Islam.[2] He means as well any form of narrow self-justifying dogmatism. In the Kyoto Lecture, his view is that a significant factor leading to 'the murderous struggles that blight our world' is the motivation to establish a secure 'metaphysical' perspective on matters such as 'the search for meaning in life, or the aspiration for purity and innocence, for a cause to which one can dedicate oneself'. By being presented as 'secure', the outlook will be in permanent variance with the fluctuations and processes of real life, history, and culture.

Regarding this line of thought, the reference to 'the search for meaning' in life, meaning one's own, and understanding human life and history in the wider sense is again central to Taylor's approach, to his 'philosophical anthropology'.

---

[1] 'Block thinking and the collapse of tolerance', The *Guardian*, 17/09/2007.
[2] Taylor's 2004 essay 'Notes on the Sources of Violence: Perennial and Modern, in Taylor (2014) pp.188-213 gives the problem of violence a treatment that is consistent with the insights into the human condition found in *Sources* and *Authenticity*.

Going back to Taylor's studies of and interests in continental thought, something he takes hold of from this tradition, as well as from his training in history, is a concern for hermeneutics, for using the disciplines and methods of interpretation to unravel the puzzles and solve the problems entailed in the varied aspects of life. This concern and interest put into perspective the contrast with the trends in Oxford philosophy that Taylor found uncongenial. In that tradition, there was a tendency to use logical and grammatical analyses to define and refine exactitude and precision in the use of language so as to demarcate sense from nonsense. Taylor thinks this assumes too abstract and too reductive a sense of language and also of life.

In Taylor's work, we find the rather wider and richer view, where the perspective taken on language sees it as another phenomenon with authentic variability. Language allows 'reasoning, calculation and coordination. It has a wide range of expressive functions, it bonds us; it allows us to narrate, to create poetry'. Language is also expressive of the anthropological and social condition of humanity, a function of the embedded human condition enabling and expressing culture:

'… no-one invents language on their own; those who are not inducted into language by others remain deprived of the crucial capacities we think of as human'.

These factors challenge narrow, reductive analyses of language and provoke a wider sense of 'the whole phenomenon'. Thinking on this, Taylor's suggestions are that language might be considered to include not just 'what we call speech and derivative writing' but also 'music, mime, dancing, painting, sculpture': seeing that language is 'social and expressive' is, he thinks, of great importance in making sense of how humanity has developed and evolved.

It is a feature of this outlook that in proposing all of this linguistically, Taylor is never seriously troubled by the thought that we also use language (and thought) at a meta-level to calibrate and explore the reasoning, calculative, scientific, poetic, historical, political, technical and other varieties of language-use that are within and expressive of human life, society and culture. Taylor sees this as part of the expressive, creative and intellectual capacity of what it is to be an empowered language-using human.

At this point, we can say that with the implicit moral ontology he sees through the lens of his philosophical anthropology, Taylor puts a premium value on a certain form of reflective and discursive reasoning. He relies on this to render his studies and recommendations into a communicative and persuasive form. We will observe how such discourse is developed and defended as our study of *The Ethics of Authenticity* unfolds. However, from what we have learnt about Taylor from this chapter, it is as well to consider that the approach he has to cultivating an 'ethic of authenticity' is unlikely to follow the conventions in moral philosophy such as engaging in a metaethical analysis as a prelude to setting out some form of normative ethic.

All the evidence so far suggests that Taylor has a significant intellectual allergy against the artificiality he sees in the standard approach within the orthodox philosophical community. In contrast, he wants to provide a more descriptive diagnosis of the human condition set within historical and cultural traditions.

2. The Malaise of Modernity and The Ethics of Authenticity – Section I[1]

Introduction

As we have established, in 1991, Taylor published *The Malaise of Modernity*, a book based on a radio lecture series, The Massey Lectures. The book revealed an expansion of the original five-lecture series. Later the same year, the identical text was retitled *The Ethics of Authenticity*, when Harvard University Press published it in a compact hardback edition.[2]

The two titles offer contrasting perspectives on the book.[3]

The connotations of *The Malaise of Modernity* are immediate and ongoing, with some weight being placed on the 'malaise', suggesting, Taylor thinks, a sense in the contemporary world that some people express of 'a loss or a decline, even as our civilization "develops"' (p.1).

Taylor swiftly moves into diagnostic mode, identifying three dominant underlying causes of uncertainty and concern – the 'Three Malaises in the section's title. These malaises are, in other terms, three 'worries' (p. 2) that Taylor has about the way we are living now. Taylor explores them as the section unfolds, but in brief, the first malaise is 'individualism': this has to do with 'a loss of meaning, the fading of moral horizons' (p. 10). The second

---

[1] Quotations from *The Ethics of Authenticity* (Taylor: 2003) – will be referenced by page number within the text.

[2] As explained in Chapter 1, the layout and pagination of both books is identical. A paperback version of *The Ethics of Authenticity* was published in 2018. The audio recordings of the lectures can be found on YouTube.

[3] At the time of writing, Charles Taylor's bibliography on his web page at McGill University lists the book as *The Malaise of Modernity*.

malaise is the primacy in modernity of 'instrumental reason' (p. 5), which leads to 'the eclipse of ends' (p. 10), by which Taylor seems to mean purposes that are of deeper value to the human condition. The third malaise comes from 'the loss of freedom' (p. 9), as evident in what is termed 'soft' despotism. As we soon discover, the first malaise is given considerable investigation over the next seven sections (II-VIII). The other two are discussed much more briefly in sections IX and X.[1]

The better-known title – *The Ethics of Authenticity* – sounds as if Taylor will be expounding and defending a particular ethical approach, one orientated around 'authenticity'. Although this supposition is broadly correct, Taylor takes some time to give us insight into his view of what the 'ethic of authenticity' entails. As the points about Taylor's interests in the previous chapter indicate, we do not discover much evidence of a conventional elaboration and illustration of a specific ethic in the text. This is related to Taylor's suspicions about aspects of the philosophical tradition, harking back to his disregard for the Oxford style of philosophical analysis, and coupled with his regard for themes and approaches in continental thought; this gives scope for what Taylor calls 'philosophical anthropology'.

We could say that a part of Taylor's background and training, as well as his view that life is embedded in interactive patterns of moral evaluation, lead him to dispense with the ethical baby along with the discharged philosophical bathwater: in *Authenticity*, he does not set out an ethical theory, so much as tease out the 'ethic' of authenticity from a review and explanation of how and why we live as we do and to so pointing up how we ought to live.

It is also fair to say that in his earlier work, *Sources*, Taylor sets out in much more elaborate ways what he thinks on

---

[1] Taylor uses Roman numerals to sequence his sections.

these various matters so that when he indicates, in *Authenticity*, that he is offering a space-limited review of the issues, problems and solutions, he is, up to a point, simply telling it as it is.[1] Even so, Taylor knows that what is said in *Authenticity*, space-limited or not, has to hold together with a coherent shape and purpose.

To minimise uncertainty and to aid in getting a grasp of what Taylor is, in principle, always looking to defend, he says in Section II of *Authenticity* that within modernity, there is an aspiration for 'self-fulfilment', a form of self-development, one that involves the principle of being 'true to oneself' (p. 15).

Taylor wants to develop two lines of thought about this principle of self-development. One is that self-development in modernity has gone badly wrong through coming to expression in 'debased and travestied' forms that are various modes of self-indulgence. Despite the risk of self-indulgence, the other is that there is 'a powerful moral ideal behind self-fulfilment', and Taylor is consistently at work to promote this, the deeper and truer version. He develops this principle of self-fulfilment into the 'contemporary ideal' of 'authenticity' (p. 16). The positives associated with this ideal evoke a vision of 'what a better or higher mode of life would be'. Taylor will also show in some detail how the ideal is prone to deviant forms, but it remains the ideal he looks to renew for the 'ethics of authenticity'.

We shall look at this definition in more detail in due course, but for now, at least we can have in mind that the 'ethic of authenticity' denotes the 'moral ideal' of being true to oneself to the end of self-fulfilment. Having moral ideals that we live for is a feature of classical thought, with echoes of Plato's notion of 'the vision of the good', where the ideal

---

[1] See *Authenticity* p. 12.

49

is 'the form of the good.'[1] Time will tell if there is any resonance to this echo.[2] Nevertheless, what Taylor stresses is that the moral ideals in question give 'a picture of what a better or higher mode of life would be, where "better" and "higher" are defined not in terms of what we happen to desire or need, but offer a standard of what we ought to desire'.

With these affirmations, a range of questions are begged as to what 'better', 'higher' and 'being true to oneself' mean, and the following questions are worth keeping in mind as we proceed

What mode or shape of value is Taylor assuming here?

How are these core values defined?

Are they intrinsic to the human condition, or are they pertinent qualities acquired through life by and for the individual?

What does the life of one who is 'being true' to themselves look like?

Does it matter what they do, or is it just important that they act 'true to' themselves?

If authentic life has an associative character, and what matters is living in relation to something outside the self, how does this square with 'being true to oneself'?

Does Taylor give 'authenticity' form and substance in his text?

---

[1] Plato (2007). The phrases quoted are from 519c and 517c.
[2] As a spoiler alert see *Sources* pp. 92-98.

On 'Three Malaises'

'Three Malaises' is the title of Section I of the text. Taking the dual titles (*The Malaise of Modernity* and *The Ethics of Authenticity*) into consideration, the basic plot of Taylor's book flows with considerable momentum from the suggestion that modern life can be seen to have a core problem of crises of meaning and value that gives rise to a state of puzzlement, perplexity, uneasiness and concern. Taylor sees the problems of meaning and value as a particular problem of modernity, meaning cultural life as it has developed through the historical period of the modern age, to what it was as Taylor perceived it in 1990-91. In this modernity, a key theme identified at the heart of much social endeavour is development. The connotations of development are positive and optimistic. A key association is progress, another constructive feature with implications of creativity. With the positives of development and progress, Taylor thinks this also brings a paradoxical sense of 'loss' or 'decline' (p. 1), and here the implications are negative.

With his historical training and interests to the fore, Taylor sees the trends of development and progress for modernity as coming from the seventeenth and eighteenth centuries. However, Taylor notes that some think it is more a post-1945 phenomenon. Whatever the case, Taylor thinks there are clear themes in evidence, characteristic of the malaise of uncertainty and disquiet that he thinks is orientated around three aspects, two of which he thinks are commonly established. The third he takes as being implied by the first two.

We mentioned the malaises briefly above, but they can bear a summary outline before looking at them in greater detail.

The first malaise is a particular and prominent form of 'individualism' (p. 2) that Taylor sees as linked with 'a loss of meaning, the fading of moral horizons' (p. 10). In short, he means that, in the way we commonly live now, we are too much bound up with ourselves and have lost the plot regarding the more truly meaningful points about life. The idea is that a cluster of traditional reference points around which social and individual life had been orientated have drifted away, and not much has replaced them.

The second malaise is the primacy in modernity of 'instrumental reason' (p. 5), which means the form of calculative thinking where things are valued as means to individually satisfying ends. The idea is that we live with too great a preoccupation with what we will get to fulfil our wants, with too little concern about how we get it, and again, we have lost sight of our real needs. In Taylor's estimate, this approach leads to 'the eclipse of ends' (p. 10), meaning the purposes for life that are of deeper value to the human condition.

The third malaise comes from the 'loss of freedom' (p. 9), particularly through 'soft' despotism. The idea here is that in modernity, the first two malaises disempower individuals from being able to operate in relations with others so that people tend to live in a more isolated manner. State machinery and other bureaucracies, not least in the democratic mode of politics, run life on a wider scale, so for individuals, the motivation and the capacity to act is diminished and is accordingly far more restricted than we usually realise. As a result, this brings about the malaise of the 'loss of freedom' as people become imprisoned in modernity's despotic organisational political structure.

This swift portrayal makes the malaise-ridden scenario sound rather bleak. Taylor thinks it is a worry, but he also has a redemptive mission in the book. He considers that the ethical ideal of authenticity is something that can be restored, not least because he presents it as the foundation for what though the malaises are deviant variants. His point is that something can only be a deviant if there is something else from which to deviate.

We will now unpack these malaises in more detail.

Individualism

Taylor suggests that if we had considered what was 'the finest achievement' (p.2) within and for life in modern developed societies, it would be no surprise to find individualism as the emergent winner. By individualism, Taylor means the view that to be genuine and wholly fulfilled in humans terms, individuals must be free in the sense of having 'the right to choose for themselves their own pattern of life, to decide in conscience what convictions to espouse, to determine the shape of their lives in a whole host of ways that their ancestors could not control'. Taylor is alert to the condition that we have an enhanced defence of individual human rights in modernity, with liberal values that support freedom of thought and expression, freedom of conscience, and freedom of action.[1] This is linked to the legal defence of the autonomy of the individual against the traditional view, that the good life would be one of obedience to a controlling power, whether political or sacred:

'In principle, people are no longer sacrificed to the demands of supposedly sacred orders that transcend them.'

Taylor is writing almost a decade before the events of 9/11 that showed that some people were opposed to the values of liberal modernity and obedient to 'supposedly sacred orders that transcend them'. That such individuals were also rejecting the values of modernity in this way would provide

---

[1] It is fair to say that this culture of regard for liberty has been somewhat challenged recently by the ongoing rise of variants of the problems that Taylor details in his text. See Mill (1987) for the classic defence of civil and social liberty.

no consolation to Taylor. His complete commitment and style of activism involve, as he says later in the text, developing 'a work of persuasion' (p. 72). His purpose is to develop a recharged perspective that promotes greater 'responsibilization' (p. 77) – a much more congenial way than terrorism to build a case against modernity.

It is to be noted that the matters Taylor engages with are often components of what we might term political rather than ethical discourse. The analyses of the three malaises point beyond the 'matter of changing the outlook of individuals' (p. 8) to changes that are 'institutional as well'. However, this wider political interest is impregnated with moral concerns, as we shall see.

There is much of this in the line Taylor takes in arguing about the problems that can be identified with individualism, for however majestic the notion of being an individual is, the problem is that individualism has been dangerously overcooked. To unpick the problem, Taylor notes that our sense of meaning and value in the wider sense comes through participation in the social orders of life, with reference to values and norms that have a cultural range and historical depth. In contrast, if individualism becomes over-prioritised, there comes a dislocation from a structured and grounded life. This also means a dislocation from the world of values that such participation gives. The tensions here come from a duality in the notion of individualism that will run on through the reviews Taylor makes in the text. What Taylor identifies is the form of individualism that is forged through associations with others and is always responsive, relational and responsible, and another form of individualism that is identical in origin and orientation save that it is operational on a far more self-interested basis. The first form is the one that Taylor looks to endorse within the ethics of authenticity: the second form is seen as a devalued and debased variant, falling into instrumentalism, subjectivity and relativism.

Taylor argues that historical settings, and he almost seems to be thinking back towards medieval theological culture, showed a 'hierarchical order in the universe' (p. 3) and a 'cosmic order, a "great chain of Being" in which humans figured in their proper place, along with angels, heavenly bodies, and our fellow earthly creatures'.[1] This perspective, and the social orders associated with it, has been discredited by 'modern freedom', which shows that the traditional orders could be seen as restricting human liberty and development.

What Taylor means may be illustrated by imagining the comparison between living in Europe in 1450, where most individuals would be limited in terms of mobility and education, with life in the current modernity: in the latter age, the patterns and conventions of life will give individuals far more scope for personal development. Taylor knows this, and it is fair to say that he is never arguing for a regressive move back to an archaic mode of life. However, he also thinks that modern freedom has come at a cost, and, writing rather generally, he comments that 'the rituals and norms of society had more than merely instrumental significance'. He means those rituals and norms were not simply means to the end of individualism. He references Kierkegaard – who promoted greater passion for life, and Nietzsche – who was also pessimistic about the trends of modernity.[2] Taylor then alludes to the view that what has been lost is the 'heroic dimension of life' (p. 4), meaning the sense of a higher point and purpose that makes life worth living and dying for. These values are set in sharp

---

[1] Here, as quite often in this text, Taylor is drawing on his earlier *Sources*. In this case, see *Sources* pp. 274ff. The 'chain of being' has echoes of the poet Alexander Pope and will be considered in Chapter 9 below.

[2] S. Kierkegaard (1813-1855): Danish philosopher and theologian; F. Nietzsche (1844-1900): German philosopher and writer. Both thinkers are often seen as precursors of twentieth century existentialism. On Nietzsche, see Loxton (2021).

contrast with the modern focus on individualism, which promotes a heightened disposition for individual self-absorption so that our lives become 'flattened and narrowed'.

Here Taylor deploys what we will find to be favourite imagery.[1] Humanity is 'flattened and narrowed' in that we are 'poorer in meaning, and less concerned with others or society.' Perhaps having seen *Star Wars*, he says this is the 'dark side' of individualism. Developing this review, he appeals to Alexis de Tocqueville, who saw from his study of the emerging American democracy that the ethos of democratic equality was leaving governance to those elected, while the people were getting on with creating a culture of indulgence, where individuals sought vulgar pleasures and lived in a dangerous state of retreat: 'et menace de le renfermer enfin tout entier dans la solitude de son coeur' – meaning 'the menace of confining all within the solitude of one's own heart'.[2]

The ideas of de Tocqueville had, in an earlier period, a considerable influence on J. S. Mill's consideration of liberty and democratic tendencies, as in *On Liberty* (1859).[3] It is worth reflecting on the problem that Taylor is drawing out, which entails an assault on another celebrated feature of modernity, democracy.

While democracy can be presented as involving a wholesome defence of individuals and as a means of giving the best imaginable solution to principled political management, the problem is that when the democratic spirit

---

[1] We shall see in the next chapter where he gets his 'flattening and narrowing' imagery from.
[2] Here Taylor quotes from his French edition of de Tocqueville - *De la Démocratie en Amérique* (1831) See *Authenticity* p.123 n. 1. Alexis de Tocqueville (1805-1859).
[3] See for example Mill (1987) p. 62. John Stuart Mill (1806-1873). Mill wrote *On Liberty* in the 1850s and it was first published in 1859.

is embedded in social and cultural life, then the sense in which everyone counts as one, without fear or favour, means that each person has an equal entitlement to be the controller of their destiny. If they focus on this, and de Tocqueville's perception was that they did, this can lead to the reductionism through what Taylor terms 'narrowing and flattening', with individuals locked with increasing passion into their own affairs, with equality of interest neutralising anyone from pressing anyone else with an objection to their own feelings as to what is right and best for them. This builds into a reduced interest in or commitment to the social orders and to a moderation of interests and concerns, leading to a damaging mediocrity. Mill particularly develops this critique with the view that due to the growing assumption that the majority view must prevail, there is the threat of the enveloping and illiberal 'tyranny of the majority'.[1] Habitually, people are inclined to adopt unquestioningly the trends and patterns of life that emanate from the majority view. Within the developing culture of democracy, the assumption grows that majority views are to be accepted: minority views and minority-view holders become marginalised and alienated, and the liberties of thought, discussion and action are diminished and endangered.

Taylor links these sorts of difficulties with the democratic ideal and reality to an overzealous enthusiasm for a style of individualism, a matter he gives attention to in most of the rest of his book.

---

[1] Mill (1987) p. 63. I am examining Mill's ideas in a forthcoming study of *On Liberty*.

Instrumental Reason

Taylor next considers what he calls the 'primacy of instrumental reason' (p. 5) in the modern setting, meaning by 'primacy' that it is something of massive influence. By 'instrumental reason', he means 'the kind of rationality we draw on when we calculate the most economic application of means to a given end'. By 'kind' of rationality, we can assume that Taylor thinks that there are other, better styles of 'rationality', but as yet, he is not elaborating anything on this theme. By 'economic', Taylor is not thinking of economics in the sense of the intellectual discipline, so much as the everyday sense of cost-effective solutions, where such solutions are reckoned to be good.

As presented, instrumentalism is at work wherever the worth is anything is calibrated by the cost of the means to bring about the desired end. Calibrations of this type give reasoning a tight and functional focus. Thinking more widely into ethics, approaches where the means are governed by ends are found with both the pragmatic approach, which looks to see the value of anything in its practical or cost-value, and the utilitarian style, where what is good, right and just is always a matter of what corresponds consequentially to the interests, pleasure or happiness of the greatest number. Taylor thinks that when the worth of anything, or anyone, is proportional to instrumental, consequentialist, and pragmatic values, the practical outcome is that the means are invariably subordinated to the end. This means that present realities are subordinated to some future, intended but as yet still absent end. This devalues the present because the implication is that the value of everything is intrinsically neutral: the value or worth of everything is conditional on the entailment or consequence that brings about the desired outcomes relative to combinations of happiness, pleasure or interest. As Taylor puts it:

'... things... will be decided in terms of efficiency or "cost-benefit" analysis, that the independent ends that ought to be guiding our lives will be eclipsed by the demand to maximise output'.

The 'independent ends that ought to be guiding our lives' that are in danger of being eclipsed by instrumentalism seem to link to the comments we considered where Taylor outlined the 'better' and 'higher' standards of 'what we ought to desire' (p. 16). On the issues to do with instrumentalism, Taylor's explanation involves a contrast, seeing the modern trend as a reaction to the former social assumption of 'a sacred structure' (p. 5) where 'social arrangements and modes of action' were set in relation to 'the order of things or the will of God'. Now, in an age of both individualism and the moral neutralism of instrumental reason, things 'are in a sense up for grabs'. For human life, to make the point again, 'independent ends that ought to be guiding our lives' are 'eclipsed' by the economic imperatives of higher rates of production and lower costs.

It does not quite go without saying that the notion of 'independent ends' that Taylor alludes to sounds very much like something conceived as over and above or transcending the here and now of everyday life. However, Taylor does not develop an explanation of this at this stage. He continues to unpack his thoughts on the perils of instrumental reason, the culture of which entails a fixation with the development of improved or novel 'technological solutions' (p. 6), this because we can, not because we need to, or because we have come up with something that is actually better. Here, the concept of planned obsolescence lurks in the background, but in the foreground is what is cited as the 'device paradigm', a state of being where we 'withdraw more and more from "manifold engagement" with our environment' (p. 7).[1] The trend is to be immersed in products that deliver 'some circumscribed benefit'.

---

[1] Here Taylor is quoting from Borgman (1984) pp. 41-42.

Since Taylor's time of writing, technological innovation has continued with an accelerated scale and pace. From the early 1990s, the '.com' generation has seen dramatic instances of change on this model, including the 'Android' vs 'iPhone' conflicts since 2014 and the machinations over the provision of mobile networks with ever higher 'g' ratings. Taylor's point, not noticeably weakened since he wrote, is that there is a sense in which innovative change becomes an end in itself. All this leads, in social planning, to 'forms of cost-benefit analyses that involve grotesque calculations, putting dollar assessments on human lives' (p. 6). In medicine, it can result in a neglect of care for the patient: the patient should be seen 'as a whole person with a life story, and not as the locus of a technical problem'.

Taylor thinks that the dominant role of technology in our lives contributes to the 'narrowing and flattening' of life noted as a feature of individualism. It is suggested that modernity entails 'a loss of resonance, depth and richness in our human surroundings', meaning that we have somehow been logged out of the narrative background to life, which provided orientation to the individual's particularity.

Taylor again refers to Karl Marx, this time seeing him as an ally in the portrayal of modernity's transience. Interestingly, the phrase he cites from *The Communist Manifesto* – 'all that is solid melts into air' – is one Marx (and Engels) use, with a clear allusion to Shakespeare's *The Tempest*, where the character Prospero has lines that are eloquent in their expression of the finitude and impermanence of life:

'Our revels now are ended. These our actors,
As I foretold you, were all spirits, and
are melted into air, into thin air,
And, like the baseless fabric of this vision,
The cloud-capped towers, the gorgeous palaces,
The solemn temples, the great globe itself,
Yea, all which it inherit, shall dissolve,

> And, like this insubstantial pageant faded,
> Leave not a rack behind. We are such stuff
> As dreams are made on, and our little life
> Is rounded with a sleep.[1]

In their work, Marx and Engels declaim as follows:

'Constant revolutionising of production, uninterrupted disturbance of all social conditions, everlasting uncertainty and agitation distinguish the bourgeois epoch from all earlier ones. All fixed, fast-frozen relations, with their train of ancient and venerable prejudices and opinions, are swept away, all new-formed ones become antiquated before they can ossify. All that is solid melts into air, all that is holy is profaned, and man is at last compelled to face with sober senses, his real conditions of life, and his relations with his kind.'[2]

The idea that Taylor wants to press for the post-modern world is that we increasingly live in a more ephemeral age. The industrial and technological aspects have grown, impacting more on the way we shape our lives. Economies operate with the production and sale of commodities that are specifically not made to last. This is contrasted with the traditional model of artisanship, where products were crafted and had a lasting use-value.

An example Taylor gives concerns the various technologies that make heating the home a matter of flicking a switch, as opposed to the traditional activity of pioneer times in Canada, where the whole family would be engaged in the business of collecting, cutting and stacking firewood, and in building and maintaining fires. In a related sense, Taylor quotes with approval Hannah Arendt's comment on modern methods of production that, 'the reality and reliability of the human world rest primarily on the fact that we are surrounded by things more permanent than the activity by

---

[1] *The Tempest*: Act 4 Scene 1.
[2] Marx and Engels (2015) p. 6.

which they were produced' (p. 7).[1] This is related to the trend that instrumental reasoning leads to in developed societies that gives rise to the mechanisms of management that come to prominence, leading to processes where decisions are taken for impersonal reasons and for ends dictated by market forces. The economic motives of efficiency and profit are developed, rather than 'humanity and good sense'.

It could be argued that this means that humanity has become subservient to the market forces and the control of the state. If so, then Taylor approves of the phrase 'the iron cage', associated with the sociologist and philosopher Max Weber, and used to denote the characteristic fate of modernity to be captive to instrumental and technological operations.[2] As it happens, Taylor is a victim of translation, for Weber never uses the term 'iron cage'. In the 1930 English translation of Weber's *The Protestant Ethic and the Spirit of Capitalism* (1905), the phrase *stahlhartes Gehäuse* – meaning 'steel-hard housing' – is recast as 'iron cage'.

Either way, the image of metallic confinement is used to portray the restrictions of living under the rational, technological and bureaucratic systems of life, and the vagaries of translators and metallic options aside, Taylor's point is that the state of modernity shows that the 'institutional structures' (p. 8) of 'the market' and 'the state' are so strong that we seem 'utterly helpless' to resist.[3] Some radicals entertain the thought of undertaking a major restructuring to 'totally dismantle' modernity's social and

---

[1] Here Taylor quotes from Arendt (1959) p. 83. See *Sources* p. 501, where he makes the identical reference to Arendt. Hannah Arendt (1906-1975), a German-Jewish philosopher who fled Germany in 1933. She spent some years in Paris and later moved to the USA. *The Origins of Totalitarianism* (1951) and *The Human Condition* (1958) are two of her most notable writings.

[2] Max Weber (1864-1920). German philosopher and social theorist.

[3] See Weber (2005) p. 123. Taylor picks up on the idea of the 'iron cage' in Section IX of his book.

political system. This somewhat revolutionary step is dismissed as 'unrealizable' and overly pessimistic about the options for a resurgence of authenticity. Taylor moves on to promote what is the first step in constructing his positive view.

The suggestion is that criticisms that portray our capacities for improvement as limited are 'abstract and wrong' and that 'our degrees of freedom are not zero'. We are, Taylor thinks, capable of 'deliberating what ought to be our ends'. Here the important words are 'deliberating' and 'our': Taylor is not keen to offer a means of personal salvation, so much as a recipe for interpersonal and social regeneration. He wants to reset 'the outlook of individuals' towards others, and to restructure institutions.

Taylor does not immediately address these issues, but we can note that he said a little earlier that a concern was over losing 'the independent ends that ought to be guiding our lives' (p. 5). The idea of obligation alluded to recurs with the link made between 'freedom' and ends shaped by 'the point of deliberating what ought to be our ends' (p. 8). These positive references to matters of obligation reveal what the moral philosopher would see as a deontological strand in Taylor – there is what might be termed a mere smear hint of Kantian thinking here. Taylor clearly considers that obligations are significant, and in their distinct ways, both he and Kant consider that humans live and operate in relational scenarios to others, where reciprocal and dynamic interpersonal obligations are key aspects of life. For Kant, reciprocal obligations are owed to others, on the basis that 'a human being and generally every rational being *exists* as an end in itself, *not merely as a means* to be used at the pleasure of this or that will; rather, it must in all its actions, whether those are directed towards itself or also to other rational beings, always be considered *also as an end.*[1] Taylor stresses the worth of 'humanity and good sense' (p. 7) and the ideal of 'political control of our destiny', which is something 'we should exercise in common as citizens' (p. 10). He then defends the notion of 'our dignity as citizens' as a counter to the threats of the malaises.

In the text of *Authenticity,* Taylor occasionally shows, as here, some overlaps of interest with the Kantian style of ethics. However, despite his valuations of dignity, obligation, reason and freedom, Taylor does not orientate himself to the Kantian approach, which he sees as being narrowly over-theoretical and abstract, with too great an emphasis on developing notions or moral freedom into 'autonomy' (p. 28). Taylor also argues that in modernity, a significant job needs to be done to work for a reorientation in prioritising our actions and values. To a considerable extent, as we will see, Taylor intends the book to present such a reasoned reorientation.

The 'Loss of Freedom'

The matter that Taylor fixes on next is the third component, perhaps the more overtly political aspect in the malaise of modernity, the issue of a 'loss of freedom' (p. 9).

This loss is seen as arising from the trends of individualism and instrumental reason. As Taylor presents it, the first malaise involves an acute form of individualism leading to the 'atomism of the self-absorbed individual'. Taylor uses the notion of atomism to express the sense that in modernity, humans are promoted as individuals, as distinct components, thus eroding notions of civic order, obligation and social duty. The second malaise, instrumental reason, leads to humanity being over-governed by impersonal

[1] Kant (2019) p. 41. The ethical thinking of Immanuel Kant (1724-1804) famously puts emphasis on the imperatives of obligation in respect of persons considered as ends, and never only as means.

forces and becoming prone to drifting into a retreat from relational engagements, as the systems and structures that dominate the way we live inhibit our capacities and diminish our capacity for freedom.

For example, Taylor notes how, in city life, it is hard to manage without a car. This is symptomatic of how, in practical terms, our choices seem limited. We find it hard to combat problems that we know are threatening, such as those concerning environmental matters. Taylor cites a problem of topical concern, the thinning of the ozone layer. Perhaps he would now update his reference and touch on the Extinction Rebellion movement, and consider that the influences of more recent campaigns give evidence of the capacity he favours for enhanced 'persuasion' (p. 72) towards 'responsibilization' (p. 77).

Taylor's underlying point is that the way we live and how social life is organised inhibits our capacity to act differently. Taylor again refers to de Tocqueville to illuminate the residual problem humanity faces: in modernity, the sort of individuality we have means that we are too easily inclined to become 'enclosed in our own hearts' (p. 9). Following de Tocqueville's perspective, Taylor thinks that in modernity, we prefer separate private lives to engagement in social and cultural life. We become increasingly reliant on central administration and global agencies to distribute and manage the means to the end of our satisfaction.[1] Taylor suggests that this gives rise to 'soft' despotism, where – quoting de Tocqueville[2] – an 'immense tutelary power' holds sway over all of our affairs and further constrains our motives for action. It is thus that with individualism, human life experiences the atomised state of self-absorption, which disables capacity for what Taylor sees as the necessary counter, which is to engage through

---

[1] For a thoughtful review of this problematic phenomenon see Ignatieff (2001).
[2] See *Authenticity* p. 9 n. 9.

voluntary action in the day's social, intellectual and cultural affairs to regenerate 'a vigorous political culture'.

Here we have a powerful issue of concern, Taylor thinks, both for the present and what he sees as the generation ahead. Since Taylor wrote, the problem he has in mind is illustrated by the retreat by many individuals into the virtual worlds enabled by the internet and the low levels of participation in national elections in the UK and other democracies.[1] Taylor's suggestion is that the situation he describes constitutes a form of 'alienation' (p. 10), a state where humanity is in some respects detached from its true nature or potential. The means by which 'political control' is sustained so we as citizens can act to shape 'our 'destiny' and achieve control 'in common as citizens' is under threat.

What Taylor has in mind as helpful to the positive endeavours for life is 'political liberty' as defined by de Tocqueville – or, we may suggest, liberty of thought and discussion as defended by J. S. Mill in *On Liberty*. As Taylor sees it, in modernity, these themes are endangered by the impersonal forces of instrumentalism and by the misguided ethos of individualism when taken as an end in itself.

In summary, Taylor thinks that with individualism in modernity, the commitment to the development of self-discovery as against critics who seem to prefer earlier times of oppression has paradoxically led to a loss of meaning, to what some term a 'culture of narcissism' (p. 11).[2] Here Taylor seems to be anticipating the self-regard of those devoted to taking and displaying endless selfies and criticising that approach to life where the interests of the person in question are the only ones that will count. At the

---

[1] This and related problems for democracies are discussed in the final chapter below.
[2] Here Taylor is thinking of Christopher Lasch's book of 1979, *The Culture of Narcissism* – See Lasch (2018) and also *Authenticity* p. 14.

same time, there is some tension in Taylor's critique of instrumental reason. If we take into account the way such thinking has brought the wider benefit of advanced science and technology, as in improvements to medical techniques, not least in the elaboration of more sophisticated diagnostic technologies, then this form of rationality is not all bad. With such matters in mind, criticism of instrumentalism can seem reactionary and anachronistic.

However, for Taylor, the resurgent problem is that of an 'eclipse of ends' (p. 10), where these ends are going to turn out, on Taylor's scale of assessment, as more estimable ideals and values than anything eclipsing them, and together these negative trends bring about a 'loss of freedom'. This 'loss' is, in effect, a form of myopia: Taylor thinks that we have lost sight of values that we would freely choose to live in relation to, and so in modernity, although we think we are free, our true freedoms have been constrained.

Taylor refers to 'the proponents of mere negative freedom who believe that the value of political liberty is overblown' (p. 11) and who think that developments in 'scientific management' are a good thing to the end of giving 'maximum independence for each individual', thus showing that modernity has 'its boosters as well as its knockers'.

Taylor alludes to the common distinction between negative and positive freedom as classified in political philosophy. The most notable exponent in this region of thought, Isaiah Berlin, gives his deftest summary of the distinction here, terming negative liberty as the 'freedom from' the constraints of 'whatever shuts off possibilities for action that would otherwise be open'.[1] Positive liberty has to do with 'freedom to'. Our freedom or liberty is real, on

---

[1] Berlin (2017) p. 326. Berlin was well known to Taylor, have been his doctoral supervisor and his predecessor in Chichele Chair at Oxford – Berlin held this Professorship from 1965 to 1976; Taylor from 1976 to 1981. See Chapter 1 above.

this view, if, but only if, we are in all respects free from whatever might control us. Thus we must ask in all respects of our life: 'How far I am controlled?' and 'Who controls me?' With a health warning over the danger of over-generalisation, we could say that in modernity, general developments have reduced the problems of negative liberty (we have much greater freedom from restrictions), but it seems that positive liberty (the freedom to) is threatened by rafts of additional social and legal controls that inhibit.[1]

From his reference to negative freedom, one can guess that Taylor is not a great fan, and in a later essay, he develops a sustained criticism of this form of liberty.[2] This criticism is not at a developed stage in *Authenticity*: it comes in the way that what are seen as the debased versions of play too much on the themes of the virtue of negative liberty. In *Authenticity*, he is sure that there are arguments in favour (from those he again calls the 'boosters') and against (from those he calls the 'knockers'), but he is equally sure there is an argument to have to achieve a synthesis between supporters and critics of the trends he has identified. Taylor is sure that the issues are not resolvable as radical alternatives, either for or against, but through a fusion of key elements. Here Taylor has a solution that shows a form of allegiance to the Hegelian notion of synthesis.

Taylor ends the first section by saying that in what follows, he will give particular attention to the first malaise, the varied problems associated with individualism. He hopes that the line he takes in suggesting a pattern for recharging the true ideal of authenticity can be applied to the other two problems, but these will be treated more lightly. Sections II-VIII unpack the review of individualism; Sections IX covers instrumental reason, and Section X the loss of freedom.

---

[1] On more detail on these notions of liberty see Berlin (2017) pp. 166-217.
[2] See Taylor's 'What's Wrong With Negative Liberty?' in Miller, D. (Editor) (2006) *The Liberty Reader*. New York: Routledge.

Reading/Revision Questions **Section I:** *Three Malaises.*

Makes notes to define, illustrate and explain the following:

1. What does Taylor mean by 'the malaises of modernity'?

2. What worries Taylor about individualism?

3. What does Taylor say about 'modern freedom'? What is the cost of this freedom?

4. What leads Taylor to be concerned about 'an abnormal and regrettable self-absorption'?

5. How does Taylor profile 'instrumental reason'?

6. What might Taylor mean by 'the independent ends that ought to be guiding our lives'?

7. Assess how Taylor uses medicine to illustrate his presentation of instrumental reason.

8. Explain what Taylor is trying to show in his references to Marx, Borgman and Arendt.

9. Why does Taylor reject fatalism?

10. Explain why Taylor is worried about our 'loss of freedom'. Explain what he takes from the ideas of Alexis de Tocqueville.

11. What does Taylor mean by 'atomism'?

12. Taylor references the 'culture of narcissism'. What is he getting at? How does the theme of narcissism fit into what Taylor has been saying?

13. Explain why, as he concludes this section, Taylor warns against trade-offs.

14. Note any questions arising from this section that touches on matters you think Taylor will need to clarify, explain or justify later in the text.

15. Note any points that Taylor makes in this section that strikes a chord of approval and reference this as the text unfolds. Does Taylor deliver on the ideas suggested in this section?

3. On 'The Inarticulate Debate' – Section II

Taylor, Bloom and Trilling

In the second section, Taylor emphasises how the trend to enhance individualism carries the threat of a loss of meaning and, it turns out, a loss of memory in terms of a form of socio-cultural amnesia. This gives rise to the enigmatic problem characterised as the 'inarticulate debate'.[1]

Taylor starts by considering some issues provoked by Allan Bloom's *The Closing of the American Mind* (1987). When it was published, this book rapidly became a bestseller, impacting on popular and public debate in the USA.[2] Bloom was a classical scholar and academic with an interest in political thought. He had studied at Chicago, where later he taught – he also worked at Cornell, Yale and Toronto Universities. Through his time at Chicago, Bloom was influenced by the 'Great Books' programme, a view of how a university education should be organised. This put emphasis on the critical reading and study of the great primary works in the various academic disciplines.[3] In turn, this meant that secondary literature, textbooks and the like were not on the academic agenda.

By this cumulative experience, Bloom was schooled in a tradition that put a premium on disciplined critical reading, the appreciation and mastery of a tradition, and the expertise of discursive scholarship. After teaching for some thirty years in university education, Bloom noticed how the

---

[1] Here see *Sources* pp. 53-90: Chapter 3 of *Sources* is entitled 'The Ethics of Inarticulacy'.
[2] Allan Bloom (1930-1992).
[3] The Universities of Chicago, Virginia and Columbia were three institutions that promoted the 'Great Books' method, which was championed by the historian Stringfellow Barr (1897-1982), who also developed the programme at St John's College, which has centres in Annapolis and Santa Fe.

increasingly liberal ethos that emerged in the 1960s changed how university students thought and worked. As one might guess from the title of his book, he noticed some problems, and the book presented a fluent study of the outlook and methods of American students as Bloom found them by the mid-1980s.

As Taylor notes, Bloom characterised the prevalent mindset as one of 'facile relativism' (p. 13), where values were commonly assumed to be personal and guaranteed by right – this by means of a link through the accumulation of the doctrine of human rights. Issues of value, including assessments of the worth of a line of thought, a text, or anything where, as a rule, issues of interpretation might be open for review and discussion, were increasingly being taken as unarguable, as the concept of personal or subjective rights and a version of the principle of mutual respect meant that everyone was assumed to be entitled to live and think according to whatever values or views they chose and held as 'his or her own "values", and about these it is impossible to argue'.

As Bloom saw it, this outlook births a form of relativism, wherein the degree of regard for personal and mutual rights, means that the style of mutual respect disqualifies each from any criticism of anything chosen by any other. It means, we could say, that responses like "Well, that is what I think" or "That is my preference, so there we are" become rather normative preludes to scenarios where people regularly agree to differ and are disabled from registering that the differences might or do matter.

This state of affairs, as Taylor notes, 'was not just an epistemological position, a view about the limits of what reason can establish' (p. 13). It was a normative view of the moral and political disposition of the rising generation. The outcome was that an individual's values and lifestyle were seen as inoculated against criticism and inviolate. Each must live in a manner that was true to oneself, and crucially, this entails that no one can dictate another's values or lifestyle since to do so would override that person's rights. All of this can be seen as contributing to an individual's self-fulfilment, but once again, the price paid is expressed by the images of life being 'narrowed' or 'flattened' (p. 14).

It now becomes clear that Taylor's prior use of this reductive imagery comes from Bloom, who, noting how little the modern university student reads, says this:

'The loss of books has made them narrower and flatter. Narrower, because they lack what is most necessary, a real basis for discontent with the present and awareness that there are alternatives to it… Flatter, because without interpretations of things, without the poetry or the imagination's activity, their souls are like mirrors, not of nature, but of what is around.'[1]

Taylor comments briefly on other texts that similarly discuss the problems of the 'individualism of self-fulfilment'.[2] Of these, the titles of the books by Christopher Lasch – *The Culture of Narcissism* (1979) and *The Minimal Self* (1984) – particularly resonate with Taylor's review of the deviant strand of the ideal of authenticity, and we have already noted his use of the theme of 'the culture of narcissism' to characterise a negative trend in modernity.[3]

This has to do with a form of individuality that 'involves a centring on the self and a concomitant shutting out, or even unawareness of the greater issues or concerns that transcend the self, be they religious, political, historical' (p. 14). This form of individualism seeds a neutral form of relativism

---

[1] Bloom (1987) p. 61.
[2] See *Authenticity* p. 14, where he alludes to works by Bell, Lasch, and Lipovetsky.
[3] See Chapter 1 above. Se also Lasch (2018) and (1984). Christopher Lasch (1932-1994) was a Professor of History at Rochester University and a prolific critic of aspects of modernity, especially of consumerism and the self-limitation or self-minimalisation that it created.

immune to self-criticism. From these other critics and Bloom's analysis, Taylor is sure that 'the relativism widely propounded today is a profound mistake' (p. 15). One of the worst implications Taylor sees is that in this modern sense, relativism leads to 'self-stultifying' perspectives adhered to by individuals, where all views are considered dependent on personal values and preferences. The background reference to the principle of equal regard entails that all such views are equally valued. It is against the current of this modernity to invest in a register of a scale of values or a basis for a deeper sense of worth. Further, relativistic views simply are what they are – they can be affirmed, but neither refuted nor justified; they are to be registered by either commendation or rejection.

For Taylor, the residual error in this is that the focus on a defence of individual self-fulfilment means a value register that is self-related to the exclusion of the self-transcending aspects of life. Instead, self-related 'dependence' leads to elemental insecurity. It leads to people looking for help from all kinds of 'self-appointed experts and guides, shrouded with the prestige of science or some exotic spirituality.'

Taylor is keen to show that there are manifest problems here and that individuality has come to be layered with difficulties. Bloom is a noble ally in making explicit the problems, but suddenly Taylor is keen to apply the brake, and become unto Bloom as Prince Hal, on becoming King Henry V, was to Falstaff.[1] For all that he takes from Bloom, Taylor sees his rejection of modernity as too pessimistic – Bloom is thus in the camp of those Taylor classified as the 'knockers' (p. 11) – those who attack individualism for the extremes they see. These critics, and Bloom, in particular, miss that in trying 'to be themselves', individuals are in touch with 'a powerful moral ideal' (p. 15). This ideal is 'at work', even though Taylor accepts that the ideal has been

---

[1] At least as according to Shakespeare – see Shakespeare (2016) Act 5 Scene 5.

'debased and travestied', and this by the 'boosters' who have pushed individualism to extremes of subjectivity. Even so, Taylor's view is that the ideal of authenticity can nevertheless be reaffirmed.

Here we come to the points that we noted earlier, that the 'moral ideal behind self-fulfilment is that of being true to oneself'. In defending the moral ideal that is to be rescued from difficulty, Taylor takes the lead from another significant thinker, Lionel Trilling, and his book, *Sincerity and Authenticity*. This brings us to what is termed 'a specifically modern understanding' of the idea of being true to oneself and to the notion of 'authenticity' (p. 16) that Taylor follows Trilling in using.

Taylor gives distinct praise to Trilling, whose observations and insights merit far more attention than we can give them here. However, it is worth noting that at the start of his *Sincerity and Authenticity*, Trilling says that sometimes 'it is possible to observe the moral life in process of revising itself'.[1] Trilling thought that he was living in such a time in the period that he was writing for, the early 1970s. He thought that the ideal of authenticity and the process of sincerity, which is all to do with being true to one's self, was assuming greater weight for the moral life.

To illustrate this, drawing in his longstanding interests in literary culture, Trilling put emphasis on a Shakespearean character's advice, that of Polonius, in *Hamlet*, to his son Laertes:

> 'This above all – to thine own self be true,
> And it must follow, as the night the day,
> Thou canst not then be false to any man'.[2]

---

[1] Trilling (1972) p. 1. Lionel Trilling (1905-1975) was a professor of English at Columbia University for most of his career. Trilling was an outstanding literary and cultural critic.
[2] *Hamlet*, Act 1 Scene 3.

This is very much the sense of being true to oneself that Taylor likes for his notion of the ideal of 'authenticity'. We will consider Polonius' view again later. However, without providing a spoiler alert to students of *Hamlet* who have not progressed too far with the play, there is a matter to raise about any variant of the view that says that the important thing is to 'be true to yourself', for this injunction seems to carry the clear assumption truly being yourself is a good thing. Nevertheless, this is a premature assumption. One of the classic variants of this phrase comes from the Greek poet Pindar, whose challenge is 'Become him who you are'; however, he adds the important rider, 'having discovered that first'.[1]

Taylor, Trilling, and not least Polonius should bear in mind that being who you are could be good, just and beneficial to yourself and others, if, but only if, you are a person with the potential for the qualities or virtues that render you a good, agreeable, helpful and constructively stimulating person. If 'being to thine own self true' means truly being a corrupt, selfish and psychopathic self, this injunction is more problematic.

Discovering the nature and character of the individual self is something for which we require a process, and this is not one that can be undertaken in isolation. Taylor has yet to unleash how this problem can be resolved.

---

[1] Pindar, *Pythian Odes*: 2: 73, quoted in Hollingdale (1999) p. 37.

The Moral Ideal of Authenticity

We now come to something approximating to the heart of the matter in getting to grips with what Taylor has in mind with the moral ideal and ethic of authenticity. Here, and again, we will recall these points from our earlier encounter, Taylor says that by the 'moral ideal' of authenticity, he means 'a picture of what a higher or better mode of life would be, where "better" or "higher" are defined not in terms of what we happen to desire or need, but offer a standard of what we ought to desire' (p. 16).

To make sense of what the imagery here is concerned with, we have to look at something that Taylor sets out in *Sources*, where he discusses 'inescapable frameworks', which are a version of the 'inescapable horizons' that come later in *Authenticity*.[1] In his earlier and much more detailed work, Taylor says that if we operate as humans within 'a framework', this:

'… incorporates a crucial set of qualitative distinctions. To think, feel, judge within such a framework is to function with the sense that some action, or mode of life, or mode of feeling is incomparably higher than the others which are more readily available to us'.[2]

Taylor explains that he is using 'higher' in 'a generic sense' and that it covers a range of ways in which 'one form of life may be seen as fuller, another way of feeling and acting as purer, a mode of feeling or living as deeper, a style of life as more admirable, a given demand as making an absolute claim as against other merely relative ones, and so on'.[3]

Bearing these points in mind, what Taylor does in

---

[1] On these inescapable frameworks, see *Sources* pp. 3-24 and *Authenticity* pp. 31-41.
[2] *Sources* p. 19.
[3] *Sources* p. 20.

Authenticity is to engage with a tension in the countering view that individualism and the ideal of self-fulfilment can appear to be no sort of moral ideal at all. It can be manifest as 'a kind of egoism' (p. 16), as 'a species of moral laxism', as 'narcissism', 'hedonism' and 'self-indulgence'. Despite these problematic risks and perils, in the ongoing project of his book, Taylor's great thought is to affirm that there is yet real 'moral force behind notions like self-fulfilment', and with reference to the sense of 'better' or 'higher' standards, over and above 'desire or need', we have the suggestion of something 'we ought to desire' – here, Taylor's reference to obligation is a clue to the shape that the ideal and ethic of authenticity – but at this stage, we have nothing more to unpack for this core notion. That 'ought implies can' operates as a defence of rational moral freedom, and how obligations over categorical imperatives relate to treating people as ends and never as means are, again, significant within the Kantian ethical project – but Taylor remains reluctant to endorse this style of ethical reflection.

In his text, a problem Taylor picks up from Bloom is the notion of 'survivalism'. Bloom means that in modern life, the demands of success in terms of personal relationships and personal ambitions over careers overwhelm other moral aspirations. Taylor thinks this is the distinctly modern form by which people lose 'the moral force of the ideal of authenticity' (p. 17). Another problem is that if the engrained form of the ideal of authenticity is in the 'debased and travestied' form of 'soft relativism', this makes any criticism of it difficult. By default, soft relativism 'means that the vigorous defence of any moral ideal is somehow off limits'. In life under such an ethos, a person's self-affirmation of something is sacrosanct, and some thirty years after Taylor's book being published, those who criticise what a person has affirmed – their beliefs, lifestyle, gender assignation or taste in socks – is liable to be regarded as phobic or something worse.

Against such problems, Taylor wants to defend the view that there is positive moral force and value in the ideal of self-fulfilment. Again, he rehearses the view 'that some forms of life are indeed *higher* than others'. He seems to be thinking retrospectively here, but he is not as reactionary as he might appear.

If, for example, we pick on individualism and portray it as a form of egoism or self-indulgence, we could use this as leverage to move back to a version of natural law. However, Taylor does not entertain this route because if it were pursued, the conformity and obedience entailed would lead to an abandonment of a key aspect of the ideal for the ethic of authenticity, the implied allure and potency of freedom and creativity. On the other hand, Taylor signals that in the contemporary culture of mutual toleration, with the lubricant of soft relativism and egoistic individualism, there is a high risk of losing the sense of higher and better values and falling into 'the liberalism of neutrality', the view that the issue of what he good life might be is not something that can be reviewed within or by a liberal society, which on such matters must remain impartial. Taylor does not approve of such marginalisation of discussion.

In the position Taylor sketches and which he challenges, a logical problem arises: if relativism is defended as an inviolate ideal, it seems as if it must have some grounds or justification through which it can be sustained as the ideal or best system of understanding. As Taylor (and Bloom) portray it, the position of soft relativism operates on the presumption of self-validation as a move from the restrictions and limits of life under the old orders. The view emerges that nothing is needed to defend the preferred view since those views flow from the integrity of self-awareness into a stream of self-referenced preferences.

Taylor does not put it this way, but it does seem as if soft relativists, if they operate in this way, lock themselves into a cognitive vacuum: if the position is that no reason can be given to prefer any form of life, then such preferences have no rational justification: how then can we know whether a given preference is not just a whim? Moreover, if everything is a matter of taste, while this might have resonance if we are discussing what to have from a menu at a restaurant, in life more generally, something has gone wrong. If we experience unease when we hear of genocide or a mass shooting, is our dislike explained as just a feeling or merely a matter of taste?

Inarticulate Debates, Moral Subjectivism, and the Failings of Social Science

There is a clear point of tension in the review Taylor makes, and the tension is increased with his view, as we noted, that 'some forms of life are indeed *higher* than others' (p. 17).

At this point in *Authenticity*, Taylor could do to make explicit the sense he defends in *Sources* about human life, especially that of the 'ineradicable sense that human life is to be respected.'[1] The mood and weight of this view inform the idea that Taylor has of the difficulty with the contemporary idiom of authenticity: 'soft relativism' undermines the attempt to defend the higher moral ideal. To be clear, the pursuit of individualism to the point of the form of moral subjectivism is not going to square with the commitment to the sense that human life entails an obligation of mutual respect. Taylor does not spell this out at this stage in *Authenticity*. What he does suggest is that at one level of reasoning, one not seen by the soft relativist, 'there is something contradictory and self-defeating in their position, since the relativism is powered (at least partly) by a moral ideal'. The soft relativist boosterised version assumes a form of the ideal that 'sinks to the level of an axiom, something one doesn't challenge but also never expounds.'

---

[1] *Sources* p. 8.

Taylor extends this criticism. Those who inhabit life within the modern version of 'the culture of authenticity' and employ the 'liberalism of neutrality' lead to the problem that has run through the review in this section, that considerations on matters of importance for how we might best live are rendered inarticulate. The life each individual chooses is, through that choice, the best for them. The 'good life' is the life wanted and sought by each individual 'in his or her own way' (p. 18). It is this cultural scenario that results in 'inarticulacy' over a matter of vital concern. The modern ideal of authenticity is something 'its friends can't speak of' and its opponents 'slight it' – what neither can do is talk about it. Taylor's underlying purpose in *Authenticity* is to break this circle and to reactive debate.

Before fully engaging with this, Taylor identifies two more 'factors' contributing to the silence of inarticulacy. He comments on the 'hold of moral subjectivism in our culture'. Moral subjectivism is defined as 'the view that moral positions are not in any way grounded in reason or the nature of things but are ultimately just adopted by each of us because we find ourselves drawn to them'. Again, in *Sources*, Taylor provides a clear illustration of what he opposes in subjectivism. He considers the experience of 'gut' reactions and takes as an example the sense of 'nausea at certain smells or objects.'[1] The point is that the reaction of nausea is self-explanatory. If something makes us queasy is what it is – just as if something makes us sneeze – again, it just is what it is, and it cannot be right or wrong, good or bad – it does not need further 'articulation'. In contrast, the tension of a genuine 'moral case' is such that we have a just case to 'argue and reason over what and who is a fit object of moral respect.'

What Taylor assumes is that we are alert to how rational theories of moral value and views on moral realism – the

---

[1] *Sources* p. 6. Taylor reuses this example in his later essay 'Disenchantment-Reenchantment', Taylor (2014) p. 297.

idea that moral value inheres in the nature of the things we are then able to identify as 'good' – are both somewhat out of fashion. In Anglo-American philosophy, emotivism manifested the view that moral preferences were no more or less significant than matters of taste – analogous to how we might say that it is simply a matter of taste as to how we like our coffee, tea, or barley water. Pragmatists favoured the view that the worth of anything, including its moral worth, was relative to whether it worked for us as a means to an end. This gives another form of instrumentalism, akin to the utilitarians, who condition the good to whatever maximises the pleasure, happiness or interests of those concerned with the act in question. In both *Authenticity* and *Sources*, Taylor's idea is that in varied ways, these trends give rise to the trends of moral subjectivism, the liberalism of neutrality, and cumulatively, inarticulacy over matters of value. These factors manifest the deviant forms of the ideal of authenticity.

Taylor is concerned about the ease with which the contemporary culture of authenticity seems happy to dispense with reason as a factor in moral deliberation. He briefly notes those who do think that there are 'standards in reason' (p. 19), alluding to the virtue theory of Alasdair MacIntyre, rooted in a tradition that goes back to Aristotle.[1]

Taylor is alert to the view that modern virtue theorists take, which entails thinking that 'there is such a thing as human nature, and that an understanding of this will show certain ways of life to be right and others wrong, certain ways to be higher and better than others'. This line of thought is akin to the thinking of Montaigne that we know Taylor likes, and so it sounds as if the virtue approach would appeal to him. Virtue theorists also have a clear counter to the emotivists' view that there are no moral facts, thinking instead that the

---

[1] See MacIntyre (1981).

facts of life give clear evidence that, as matters of fact, some things are good or better for life than others.[1]

Although, as with Murdoch's thought considered earlier, the virtue approach would appear to cohere with Taylor's thought and interests, he shows no explicit urge to link himself with the insights arising from this source, remarking that moral subjectivism – the moral subjectivism he is no supporter of – is 'very critical' of the virtue line of thought, as Aristotle's 'metaphysical biology' (p. 19) is 'out of date' and 'unbelievable'. He also thinks that the virtue tradition is critical of 'the ideal of authenticity' on the grounds that it makes the mistake of trying to base values on something other than 'the standard rooted in human nature'. Here Taylor seems to side with something he disapproves of – moral subjectivism – in supporting a view that seems to embrace the genetic fallacy: Aristotle on morality must be dismissed because of his 'unbelievable' biological theories – even though virtue theory has, as much as Taylor wants, a view of human life where, as a matter of fact, values are embedded in what it is to be human.[2] This line of thought is not one of Taylor's most compelling arguments.[3]

Taylor's outlook emerges at this stage as something of a puzzle. He might be thought to have a view about the human condition with kinship to the relational social strands of ethical thinking that modern virtue ethicists promote – but he rejects allegiance to this view, but for rather weak reasons. Taylor gives some importance to obligation, a hint of regard for some kind of neo-Kantian obligation – but as we again notice, he does not develop any commitment to Kantian ethics – he holds the ground with his commitment

---

[1] On this see Foot (2003). I have written in the issues here separately – see Loxton (2021) Chapter 17.

[2] Here again, see Foot (2003).

[3] As we will see later – in Chapter 13 – Taylor thinks more highly of this tradition in *Sources*, where he uses themes from Murdoch to underpin and express some of his main thoughts on moral ideals.

to philosophical anthropology and to the views that are related to the phenomenological style that informs his philosophical anthropology.

Given that we said at the outset of our review of Taylor's 'ethic of authenticity' that we needed to clarify the form and content of this ethic, what we can say at this stage is that Taylor is not only not developing a conventional moral philosophy along lines that seem congenial to this outlook; he is also keeping his cards close to his chest in his operation as a philosophical anthropologist. So far, we have not been told too much on the positive front. Ideas that might be helpful are alluded to but not detailed. We know that subjectivism is to be challenged and that there is an affirmation of higher and better standards that 'we ought to desire' (p. 16), but we are short on the form that a life of authenticity ought to have. On the bright side, we know that Taylor is not a resurgent Kantian and that he is not keen to endorse the virtue tradition.

The issue that Taylor is left with has a great deal to do with his own sense of how reason operates within and for the ethics of authenticity. He wants to argue 'in reason', as he puts it, for core, residual values as the basis for the ethics of authenticity, so this rather assumes that he must have a view about what and how it is that the individual can cultivate self-fulfilment. If he does not want to develop Kant's views or side with the modern virtue ethicists, he needs an explicit alternative that ties with the line of his thoughts in *Sources*, where he builds to the view that human life and thought generates 'rather massive commitments in benevolence and justice.'[1] He is otherwise caught in the snare of authenticity as an aspiration for individuals who are to be true to themselves, which as a stand-alone affirmation would seem prone to lead to the relativity and ethical neutralism that he sees as deviant forms of the ethical ideal of authenticity.

---

[1] *Sources* p. 518.

At the hub of the enterprise that Taylor is developing in *Authenticity* is the alternative argument that the trend to soft relativism and neutrality is the true pattern of the active mode of being true to oneself. To rebrand and relaunch an ethic of authenticity with a more positive approach to human association still needs the provision of a more explicit view of that in virtue of which authenticity enhances the human condition without the trends that seem to Taylor to be debased travesties of the ideal.

Taylor's solution to the problems here and his confidence in the capacity humans have to use and respond to reasoned arguments are based on the ideas he cultivated in his student years. As we found earlier, Taylor had several objections to the pattern of philosophical endeavour he found at Oxford and discovered something more persuasive in the phenomenological and existential traditions of continental thought. We have noted the ideas of Heidegger and the notion that the human reality is residually that of 'being-in-the-world', and Taylor draws on this type of thinking to ground his view that reasoning about reality is a genuine option.

We see this in something that he says in a later essay, 'Disenchantment-Reenchantment'.[1] In this piece, he makes a critical diagnostic on the epistemological tradition, with reference to Descartes' promotion of subjective reason and John Locke's subjective empiricism. Taylor thinks on this matter in *Sources* and says that these lines of thought offer positive contributions to the ongoing tradition, but whatever the other benefits they offer, they both 'generated a view of knowledge as a correct portrayal of external reality residing in the mind.'[2]

The idea here is that in some manner, varied in format between the rationalists and the empiricists, what we have subjectively in the mind is a representation of reality, a

---

[1] See Taylor (2014) pp. 287-302.
[2] Taylor (2014) p. 293-294.

85

construct and portrayal. Explaining the issues at stake, Taylor shows how the philosophical tradition generates an approach to the questions of perception and knowledge that creates a combative tension.

On the one side, we have the traditional approach to reality that has a referential character, whereby we are seen as being the 'contemplators of order'. We are in a passive, subordinate position and our insights are derivative, coming from an external authority. This is contrasted with the newer line of thought as informed by Descartes and Locke. On this view, our sense of reality is brought about by us, by the operations of mind and sensation. Taylor knows, but does not worry about, the differences between the rational Descartes and the empirical Locke: in both philosophies, what happens is that we 'construct a picture of things following the canons of rational thinking.'[1] Taylor is most emphatic in prioritising Descartes as the perpetrator of the most worrying of turns of thought. We saw earlier how Heidegger also had this concern, which amounts to the view, as Taylor puts it, that it is Descartes above all who alters the relation of 'subject and object'.[2] In the classical

---

[1] *Sources* p. 168. Descartes produced a number of important works, of which the *Discourse on the Method of Properly Conducting One's Reason and of Seeking the Truth in the Sciences*, (1637), and *Meditations on the First Philosophy in which the Existence of God and the real Distinction between the Soul and Body of Man are Demonstrated*, (1641) are the most important. The *cogito* emerges as a thought experiment, as Descartes thinks on what can provide the strongest basis for true knowledge. Our sense-experiences are unreliable, our consciousness too can deceive us; our sense of reality could conceivably be a cosmic confidence trick. Thus we have to doubt everything. Descartes then separates the objects of doubt from the act of doubting, which is an act of thought. This proves that thinking, which, Descartes considers, proves personal existence – *cogito ergo sum* – is a stronger basis for knowledge and the way that we make sense of our sense, consciousness and reality. John Locke (1632-1704) is best known for *An Essay Concerning Human Understanding* (1689), which expounds an empirical view of knowledge, and, for political thought, the *Second Treatise of Government* (1689).
[2] *Sources* p. 188.

world view, all the particulars, including individuals, existed in a relationship of dependency upon the universals. In the developing Christian world view, human life was conceived as a consequence and expression of the will of God. Taylor thinks that 'the modern idea of a subject as an independent existent is just another facet of the new strong localization.'

This new view changes our thinking and our whole conceptual map of reality, as we now think of 'ideas' as being 'in' this 'independent being, because it makes sense to see them as here and *not elsewhere*'. We no longer discern ideas; we have them. To make the point clear, Taylor contrasts the Platonic and Cartesian perspectives: for Plato, 'ideas are ontic, the basis of reality': for Descartes, ideas 'are the contents of the mind'.

Whatever benefits the modern turn of thought bring, Taylor's view is that what is imported is a clear sense of a gap between the subjectivity of representative knowledge and the objective condition of reality. The alternative is not naïve realism, the view that we see, hear, taste, touch and feel things directly as they are. What Taylor thinks more convincing is what re-emerges in the phenomenological and existential style of continental thinking of the later period, where what he notices is something of a corrective in the form of a more participatory view:

'Our grasp of the world is not simply a representation within us. It resides rather in our dealing with reality. We are being in the world (Heidegger's *Inderweltsein*), or being to the world (Merleau-Ponty's *être eu monde*).'[1]

This perspective is not explicit in any heavily underlined way in *Authenticity*, but it informs Taylor's outlook in this as in his other writings. Taylor operates on the view that to be human is to be embedded within and as a part of reality.

---

[1] Taylor (2014) p. 294.

It follows that when we reason, we think within and as a part of reality, and especially that part of reality that is social, communal and cultural. This is linked to Taylor's sense of how the project of moral philosophy should be ordered. He makes this explicit in *Sources*, and again, the ideas infuse the thinking in *Authenticity*. In the earlier work, Taylor says that in contrast to the moral philosophy in 'the English-speaking world', which has 'given such a narrow focus to morality' and 'accredited a cramped and truncated view of morality', he aims to work 'towards enlarging our range of legitimate moral descriptions, and in some cases retrieving modes of thought and description that have misguidedly been made to seem problematic'.[1] The ideas here provide something by way of an operational ontological perspective to empower Taylor's confidence in *Authenticity* that there is scope for progress to defend the ideal of authenticity.

Taylor's next issue is that on the assumption of relativism, which he does not accept, we could argue that 'reasoning' is never more than 'reasoning-relative-to' the culture, tradition or discipline of study in question. Taylor's aim, to argue for the ethics of authenticity, requires a means of showing that a form of generic reasoning is possible to critique relativism and the 'inarticulacy' (p. 18) of modernity.[2] Again, seeing and assessing how he does this is an ongoing task.

Turning briefly to the social sciences, with sociology and psychology in mind, Taylor thinks that in modern applications, their explanations contribute to obscuring the true ideal of authenticity by working instrumentally and descriptively through models that are functional or operational, relating to such trends as social mobility, urbanisation, occupational patterns and so on. There is no agenda in this activity for moral ideals and so no vocabulary

[1] *Sources* p. 3.
[2] For more on this see *Sources* Chapter 3.

88

for them. Individualist and instrumental reasons are explained as 'by-products of social change' (p. 20). Factors such as 'industrialization', social mobility, and 'urbanization' are bound up with this, leading to analyses of the human condition that focus on issues of aspiration for those at work to achieve better pay, more possessions and an enhanced lifestyle. Within such a view, freedom 'allows you to do what you want, and the greater application of instrumental reason gets you more of what you want, whatever that is' (p. 21).

Taylor sees that these trends 'thicken the darkness around the moral ideal of authenticity'. The problem is that critics disparage what they view as 'a non-moral desire' for uninhibited satisfaction; defenders are, as we have seen, 'pushed into inarticulacy about their own outlook'. The 'general force of subjectivism in our philosophical world and the power of neutral liberalism intensify the sense that these issues can't and shouldn't be talked about'. These forces fuse to put a cloak of silence around serious discussion of the moral ideal of authenticity, and the social sciences propose that the elements of human life should be explained in terms of 'changes in the mode of production, or new patterns of youth consumption, or the security of affluence.'

Earlier, Taylor remarked that the modern ideal of authenticity had been 'debased and travestied' (p. 15). He has been holding on to this point, and now he sets out the implication. What the knocking critics, notably Bloom, have been attacking are, Taylor claims, 'debased and deviant forms of this ideal' (p. 21). These devalued forms flow from a basis in the ideal of authenticity, but they misrepresent it. Bloom is cited as seeing that even soft relativism is seen 'as a moral postulate' as 'the condition of a free society'.[1]

Taylor argues that developed, soft relativism 'travesties and

---

[1] Bloom (1987) p. 25, quoted in *Authenticity* p. 21.

eventually betrays' (p. 22) the moral insights of the ideal of authenticity. Accordingly, he wants to work in the name of that ideal to reject the deviant forms. To this end, he urges the need to recover a sense of the original moral motivation and the grounds for authenticity: the project going forward is to engage in some intellectual archaeology to work up an explanation and defence for the moral ideal of authenticity and challenge and critique the 'soft relativism' and subjective individualism of modernity, both of which are considered to be distortions of the ideal of authenticity.

On this matter, Taylor insists that the ideal must be distinguished from the distortion to avoid its loss. The ideal, we must assume, is something Taylor considers worth preservation and renewal. The ideal can be emphasised, he suggests, by relating it to the things that are to do with authenticity but which are also self-transcending. Thus we need 'the past', or culture, 'the demands of citizenship', 'the duties of solidarity' and 'the needs of the natural environment'. None of these are merely instrumental means to authenticity – and we shall see later that these are variant 'horizons' that are said to be 'inescapable.'[1] Here, in a bit of a rush, we receive from Taylor more by way of a scheme for the ethical ideal of authenticity.

In the face of 'inarticulacy' he has explained, and with his scheme in mind, Taylor wants to develop greater 'articulacy' to retrieve the ideal of authenticity. He delivers his statement of intent:

'What I am suggesting is a position distinct from both boosters and knockers of contemporary culture. Unlike the boosters, I do not believe that everything is as it should be in this culture. Here I tend to agree with the knockers. But unlike them, I think that authenticity should be taken seriously as a moral ideal. I differ also from the various middle positions, which hold that there are some good things in this culture (like greater freedom for the

---

[1] See *Authenticity* Section IV and Chapter 5 below.

individual), but that these come at the expense of certain dangers (like a weakening of the sense of citizenship), so that one's best policy is to find the ideal point of trade-off between advantages and costs… The picture I am offering is rather that of an ideal that has degraded but that is very worthwhile in itself, and indeed, I would like to say, unrepudiable by moderns. So what we need is neither root-and-branch condemnation nor uncritical praise; and not a carefully balanced trade-off. What we need is a work of retrieval, through which this ideal can help us restore our practice… To go along with this, you have to believe three things, all controversial: (1) that authenticity is a valid idea; (2) that you can argue in reason about ideals and about the conformity of practices to these ideals; and (3) that these arguments can make a difference' (p. 22-23).

There are two important points to note from this passage.

Firstly, we see that Taylor is advocating a policy of restoration, of 'retrieval', as he puts it – to go with the sense of his work as one of 'persuasion' (p. 72) and to achieve the 'conformity of practices to these ideals' (p. 23), which is slipped in as the longer-term aim. Here he is recapturing a major strand in the enterprise of *Sources*. He concludes that much longer book with the view that this too was a work 'of retrieval, an attempt to uncover buried goods through rearticulation'.[1] What Taylor has in mind is that this project of restoration is related to the issue of individualism, the first malaise, but in principle, it is also to be applied to the other malaises.

Secondly, Taylor provides three points by way of a conclusion to the section: these can be restated:

1). You have to believe that authenticity is a valid ideal.
2). You have to believe that you can argue about ideals and the practices that would be consistent with them.
3). You have to believe that the argument will make a difference.

---

[1] *Sources* p. 520. See also p. xi.

Taylor will return to the broader issues here in Section VII. Meanwhile, Sections III to VI involve his investigations, and he starts by looking at the origins of the ideal of authenticity. As we trace his deliberations, we will note that he consistently affirms belief in the validity of authenticity as an ethical ideal. The more engaging matter will be to note the strength and effectiveness of Taylor's arguments to defend and develop his positive views so as to avoid the threat of what he sees as deviation.

***Reading/Revision Questions* Section II:** *The Inarticulate Debate.*

Makes notes to define, illustrate and explain the following:

1. This section starts with reference to the work of Allan Bloom. What does Taylor want to highlight in Bloom's work?

2. How, from Bloom and others, does Taylor characterise relativism?

3. How is this relativism related (allegedly) to the individualism Taylor described in Section I?

4. What is the 'powerful moral ideal' which is at work in the relativism which Bloom critiques?

5. What does Taylor take from the work of Lionel Trilling?

6. How does Taylor develop the point that there is moral force 'behind notions like self-fulfilment?

7. Make a clear summary of the key ideas that profile the 'moral ideal' of 'authenticity'.

8. What does Taylor see as the problem with 'soft relativism'?

9. How does the 'liberalism of neutrality' link to some thinkers wanting 'to banish discussions about the good life to the margins of political debate'?

10. How does Taylor explain the inarticulacy alluded to in the title of the section?

11. What is moral subjectivism? What problems are to be found with reasoning about or against this idea?

12. Why, according to Taylor, does the normal fashion of social science research obscure the importance of authenticity as a moral ideal?

13. What advantages come from explanations which focus on 'non-moral' motivations?

14. Why does Taylor think that 'the affirmation of the power of choice as itself a good to be maximized is a deviant product of the ideal'?

15. Why does Taylor claim that his proposal is not 'a carefully balanced trade-off'?

16. What three things does Taylor ask us to believe so as to engage in the 'work of retrieval' of the ideal of authenticity?

4. On *'The Sources of Authenticity'* – Section III

The Background to the Rise and Fall of Authenticity

At the start of *The Ethics of Authenticity*, Taylor ruminates on the range of options that he says are given for the period during which the sense of the modern ideal of authenticity has been developing, running, and, in various ways, going wrong. Some think it is a post-1945 phenomenon; other suggestions go back to the seventeenth century.[1] At the start of section III, Taylor comes clean and tells us what he really thinks, and in considering the sources for the moral ideal of authenticity, Taylor's further purpose is to show how the ideal of authenticity is valid, as consistent with the checklist given at the end of the preceding section. As we shall see, Taylor calls in some significant figures from intellectual history to populate the story of the origin and development of the ideal of authenticity.

As Taylor sees it, the origins of authenticity as 'something relatively new and peculiar to modern culture' (p. 25) have two initiating lines towards modernity. One, which is broader, emerges in the late eighteenth century. We would usually term this the period of the Enlightenment. However, that this an emergence in the late eighteenth century implies an earlier influence, and Taylor then moves back in time, turning again to Descartes, who contributes a key component with the notion that humans have 'disengaged rationality'. Here Taylor, who is, as we have seen, critical of aspects of Descartes's influence, finds a more positive theme to aid his project.[2] He wants a form of rationality as a primary feature of authenticity, one that is richer in potential than the instrumental mode of reasoning of which he has been so critical. Descartes' development of the line

---

[1] See *Authenticity* p. 1.
[2] See Chapters 1 and 2 above where Taylor finds some problems in Descartes' influence. See *Sources* pp. 143-159 where Taylor gives Descartes' 'disengaged rationality' an extended review.

of dispassionate thinking that Taylor calls 'disengaged rationality fits the bill. His idea is that through the power of considered rational explanation, it will become possible to expose the debased inarticulacy of the contemporary form of the ideal, where, as in the culture of subjectivism, reason is swamped by the forces of personal feeling. To this end, Taylor highlights how Descartes' *cogito* shows how human reason can 'disengage' from personal feeling, history, tradition and society, and can elaborate by its own force, criteria for truth and knowledge. It also empowers the human 'to think self-responsibly for him- or herself'. What Taylor wants to take from Descartes' insight is that human thinking involves what we might call self-critical objective reasoning, linked to our capacity to live under the idea of possessing 'moral instincts' relating, we may be sure, to Taylor's view of our shared and 'ineradicable sense that human life is to be respected'.[1]

To enrich the sense we have of the capacity for disengaged and self-responsible reason, Taylor adds elements from the political liberalism of Locke. Locke is another philosopher he is not uncritical of, but he thinks that we derive the important idea of the individual as the key political and ethical agent from him.[2] Locke's idea is that the individual will is prior to, and makes credible, the various duties and obligations individuals have in ethical and political life. From this comes the view that humans have an intrinsic capacity for moral judgment; they have 'an intuitive feeling of right and wrong' (p. 26). Taylor develops this as a counter to the instrumentalist view 'that knowing right from wrong was a matter of calculating consequences'.

Here Taylor has several things in mind: religious views of 'divine reward and punishment', and his reference to understanding values not being a matter of 'dry calculation'

---

[1] *Sources* p. 8.
[2] Taylor's thinking on Locke is given fuller treatment in *Sources* – see *Sources* pp. 159-176.

is also an anti-utilitarian point. What he does not reflect at this stage is the always tricky matter of justifying appeals to moral intuition. It is notoriously easy to say that something is 'good' or 'right' through one's moral intuition. However, someone else can say with as much intuitional sense that the 'something' in question is 'bad' or 'wrong'. To tie this up, we need to be clear that the role of disengaged rationality has to be the primary method to discern and validate moral intuitions, or we risk a variant of the retreat to subjectivism and inarticulacy.

Taylor passes on hammering home this solution and considers others who are source figures for the ethical ideal of authenticity.

The Influence of Romanticism: Rousseau and Herder

From the sources of Descartes and Locke, Taylor adds influences from the Romantic movement.[1] The idea he is keen on is that of how humans acquire a distinct ability to reason with disengaged objectivity, and to think and act in a self-responsible manner, drawing on intuitive feelings of right and wrong, with morality as 'a voice within'.[2]

Here, in a brief few passages, Taylor is engineering some very important elements in his presentation of the origins of the ethic of authenticity: we have the component of 'disengaged rationality' (p. 25), and to this, we add from Romanticism the element of feeling. Taylor likes this alliance because he sees in Romanticism a cultural influence rich in the sense of embracing the organic unity of life. He is keen on this theme, as it is a major aspect of the case he wants to make to build more participatory ways of doing life to counter the later atomism of the devalued modern version of 'being true to one's self' (p. 15).

---

[1] Usually this thought to cover the late eighteenth and early-to-mid nineteenth centuries.

[2] For more detail on this, see *Sources* Chapter 15.

Taylor makes one other vital point. The 'voice within' (p. 26) has a deeper moral significance through what is termed 'a displacement of the moral accent' of the 'notion of authenticity'. Taylor means there is a sense in which our 'being in touch with our moral feelings' achieves the 'displacement of the moral accent' as our 'being in touch takes on independent and crucial moral significance'. What Taylor means is that the independence that comes with the displacement is aided by the incorporation of 'disengaged rationality' (p. 25). The 'displacement' is from our feelings being wholly and completely orientated to our subjective interests – an orientation that would run on to the deviant form of the ideal. The point is that we experience the sense that the moral aspect is of worth over and above its being a part of our own experience.

With this combination of reason and accented feelings, the Romantic vision challenges the atomised individualism of modernity as it suggests a tie between the individual and others, and with humanity and the wider reality. Taking these elements into account, Taylor thinks that to be a 'true and full human being' (p. 26), there has to be a fusion of the inner sense of our feelings and the capacity for reasoning so that we establish 'a means to the end of acting rightly' – another deontological strand in Taylor's ethical spectrum. This fusion provides such means as Taylor suggests to moderate the vacillations risked in appeals to moral intuition or pure feelings alone, as noted earlier.

The ethic of authenticity proposed is, in some respects, in contrast with traditional approaches to morality, which, whether philosophical or theological, suggest that the individual is somehow in touch with and obedient to a source or root of the ideal or true 'good'. Thus we might have 'in earlier moral views' the sense of 'being in touch with… God, say, or the Idea of the Good'. On either the theological or Platonic ticket, the worth of an individual is defined through their correlation to the source of the ideal.

The rise of subjectivity in the modern era – 'the massive subjective turn of modern culture', as Taylor puts it, means that the core source of meaning and value comes in the guise of 'a new form of inwardness' that lies deep within us, and that we are also bonded within wider realities is the safety-net we should use to avoid the fall in the deviant form of the ideal.

As far as wider realities are concerned, Taylor has still in mind 'whatever transcends the self' (p. 22) and has weight for informing authenticity: 'our past', 'the demands of citizenship', the 'duty of solidarity' and 'the needs of the natural environment'. Taylor does not recapitulate these elements at this stage, nor does he preclude a theological view as a possible wider reality. What he does instead is to turn to another key player in the development that he charts, Jean-Jacques Rousseau.[1]

Taylor comes to Rousseau not because he is taken to be the creator of the ethic of authenticity or the inventor of subjectivism, but because he is a thinker who articulates a sense of the transition from one structure of meaning and value to another. Taylor argues that for Rousseau, the 'issue of morality' is to do with 'our following a voice of nature within us' (p. 27). The focus of self-devotion here is in tension with our feelings of 'dependence on others', which can be so great that we are led to negate our true rational selves. The key passion that can deflect us is 'amour propre', or pride. Rousseau's solution is that he urges a reconnection with our true selves to obtain contentment and joy – 'le sentiment de l'existence'.[2]

Taylor takes from Rousseau a principle of self-determining freedom, the form of freedom in the sense of 'I am free when I decide for myself what concerns me, rather than

---

[1] Jean-Jacques Rousseau (1712-1778).
[2] Here Taylor quotes from his French edition of Rousseau – see *Authenticity* p. 27 n. 21.

being shaped by external influences'. Taylor likes this to fuel his opposition to narrower theories of determinism. In effect, Taylor is contrasting a vision of self-responsible authentic selfhood with heteronomy – the condition where individuals live under the control of others. Gearing up to make another point against a certain view of liberty, he also thinks that what he is promoting involves 'a standard of freedom that obviously goes beyond what has been called negative liberty where I am free to do what I want without interference from others because that is compatible with my being shaped and influenced by society and its laws of conformity'. In contrast, self-determining freedom within the ideal of authenticity 'demands that I break the hold of all such external impositions and decide for myself alone'. That humans possess the capacity for disengaged rationality, as derived from Descartes, remains a core component in the range and power of this emerging individualism.

Taylor assumes that self-determined decision-making will be critically evaluative so that what is decided by the self is better, and as noted, linked to 'acting rightly'. He says that for Rousseau, the idea of self-determining freedom assumes a political form 'in the notion of a social contract state founded on a general will' (p. 28) – an allusion to Rousseau's famous book of 1762, *The Social Contract*. Taylor points out the now commonly made judgment that the general will expresses a view of the common will of humanity as an abstract principle; it thus turns out to be a key source for later totalitarianism. He also notes that self-determining freedom is interpreted in 'purely moral terms' by Kant in terms of autonomy and that with Hegel and Marx, the principle returns to the political dimension of life in a much more dangerous form. Self-determining freedoms in all these forms are, Taylor thinks, deviant forms of the ethic of authenticity.[1]

In contrast, what Taylor is after is an ethically more poised form of self-determination, and to this end, he pays respects to Johann Gottfried von Herder.[2] Herder is commended for promoting the idea that it is in the capacity of each and every human individual to be a unique manifestation of what it is to be human. Herder is a less well-known philosopher than he might be, perhaps because he avoided writing systematic monographs of unreadable density. His talent for fluent writing encouraged him to use essays and reviews to explore and promote his many and varied ideas.[3] Taylor likes the insight that suggests that each person 'has an original way of being human' (p. 28); thus, each person has his or her own 'measure'. In *Sources*, Taylor similarly reviews Herder to emphasise the wider point Herder took, extending individual originality to suggest that 'the locus of sovereignty must be a people', and that 'each people had its own way of being, thinking and feeling'.[4] The idea about the power of individuality is something that is explored with greater confidence through the whole Romantic movement, and indeed in the thought of Nietzsche, as the view that each person, due to their individual creative capacity, must take

---

[1] We can infer from this why Taylor is not keen on alliances with Kant. Taylor sees Kant as promoting autonomy, and does not give much weight to the more interpersonal ethic in Kant's ethical project. Arguably, Taylor takes an over-narrow view of Kant, whose critical rationalism is a model of disengaged rationality.

[2] Johann Gottfried von Herder (1744-1803).

[3] Herder's thought and influence is given full measure in Michael Forster's entry in the on-line Stanford encyclopaedia of Philosophy: see Forster, Michael, "Johann Gottfried von Herder", The Stanford encyclopaedia of Philosophy (Summer 2019 Edition), Edward N. Zalta (ed.), URL =
<https://plato.stanford.edu/archives/sum2019/entries/herder/>. Forster is also the translator and editor of Herder (2002), a very helpful collection of Herder's philosophical essays and reviews. See also *Sources* pp. 368-372.

[4] *Sources* p. 415.

as an imperative the principle that they must be true to themselves, rather than living in any way that involved conformity with or imitation of others.

A highly charged personal or individual imperative emerges here. Taylor puts the case as follows, echoing, perhaps unwittingly, a song made famous by Frank Sinatra:

'There is a certain way of being human that is *my* way. I am called upon to live my life in this way, and not in imitation of anyone else's. But this gives new importance to being true to myself. If I am not, I miss the point of my life, I miss the point of what being human is for *me*' (p. 28-29).[1]

Taylor revises this as the 'principle of originality' (p. 29) to stress that 'each of our voices has something of its own to say'. The concern is that this capacity is diminished, distorted or even lost within the commitment to self-related instrumental reasoning – where the person subordinates the here and now for the sake of something yet to be – and through conformity to external authority. Thus the 'background understanding to the modern ideal of authenticity' is seen in terms of self-authentication through being true to one's originality. The inherent sense of having within oneself the capacity to authenticate through one's own feelings and choices underpins the principle of originality.

---

[1] The singer Frank Sinatra (1915-1998) released 'My Way' in 1969 and the song, originally written in French, became an instant classic. It can be found easily on YouTube - https://www.youtube.com/watch?v=0_kG4uQI98U.

Issues Arising

Arising from this review, there are two matters to clarify.

The first has to do with Herder's development of the idea of each person being a distinctive, original instance of what it is to be human. It is important to clarify that this comes from his historical and cultural views, which suggested that the ideals and values expressed in language were relative to historical periods and specific cultures. This meant it was untenable to assume commonality over what it was to be human, not that this stopped many other theorists trying to argue otherwise. Herder suggests a pluralistic view of culture and history, and in effect, he has the insight that would easily make sense of the plural multiculturalism of modern developed societies. Herder did not argue for the liberalism of neutrality, however, as he considered that with careful hermeneutics, it was possible to discern and engage with the varieties of pluralism. He employs a variant of disengaged critical rationality, as befits a former student of Kant. Herder's idea of each individual being a unique and original instance of what it was to be human is also a remarkable anticipation of Darwinian thinking, and it is, as Taylor suggests, a very significant contributor to the emerging sense of the moral ideal of authenticity.

The second point arises around what Taylor has been constructing. If we claim to have an ethic of authenticity, and that ethic is grounded in the form of the principle of originality, then the claim sounds reversible: 'originality' equals 'authenticity'. There is an assumed, affirmed continuity of value here somewhere, but what we need to clarify is where in this resides the ethical value that justifies the correlation between originality and authenticity. On the face of it, a person could be as true to themselves as possible and be originally authentic – or authentically be very original – but what is the link that makes this moral as in the sense of 'a means to the end of acting rightly' (p. 26)? We need to recall the implicit incorporation of disengaged rationality within authenticity and the notion of the displaced accent of moral feelings that can be linked to the sense in each individual of their capacity for an original take on what it is to be human. These components, rather rapidly sketched by Taylor, help to make a very plausible outline model for the ethical ideal of authenticity.

From this, we can say that in the exposition of _The Ethics of Authenticity_, in the quest to secure a grasp of the form and content of this ethic, we have so far from Taylor an emerging outline: we have the proposal of the governance of disengaged rationality enmeshed with the capacity for self-responsibility, and we can be drawing on our morally accented intuitive feelings of right and wrong linked to the principle of originality. We have a good sense of the form, if not the detailed content for the ideals of the ethic of authenticity.[1] However, with the ideas presented so far, one thought arising is that Taylor's sense of the authentic ideal is, by default, orientated around perspectives that give the shape and form of an ethical outlook. The creativity and originality of this ethic, and so the content, are probably to be built through the activity of an authentic life in relationships, with others and with the wider world around us.

***Reading/Revision Questions Section* III: *The Sources of Authenticity*.**

Makes notes to define, illustrate and explain the following:

1. What does Taylor want to make use of with his references to Descartes and 'disengaged rationality'.

---

[1] See the Introduction, above.

2. What does Taylor think is significant about our 'being in touch with our moral feelings'.

3. What is Taylor's view of the 'new form of inwardness' which comes about with the modern age?

4. How is Jean-Jacques Rousseau seen to contribute to the evolving ideal of authenticity?

5. What contributions are made by Johann Gottfried von Herder to the ideal of authenticity?

6. Looking back over the Section, collect all the material you can on the idea of 'self-determining freedom'. Why might it be a high-risk option within Taylor's hopes for the ethics of authenticity?

5. On 'Inescapable Horizons' – Section IV

The Vitality of Reason

'Inescapable Horizons' is an evocative title, recalling the points made in Section II on the matters that transcend the self (p. 22), and we mentioned the version in *Sources* – 'inescapable frameworks' – in Chapter 3 when discussing the moral ideal of authenticity. However, Taylor does not reference any horizons at all at the start of the section.[1] Instead, he works on from other strands from the previous discussion. Having outlined key features of the ideal of authenticity and set out a fusion of reason, morally accented feelings and creative originality (pp. 26-29), Taylor picks up on an idea implied at the end of Section II (p. 23), the problem of reasoned dialogue with those who reside in the allegedly distorted contemporary mode of authenticity. Where such a state is grounded in 'soft relativism', the question is that of whether this perspective inoculates individuals against having a genuine capacity for critical self-reflection. In a rhetorical form, we have the question of whether one can 'say anything in reason to people who are immersed in the contemporary culture of authenticity?' (p. 31).

Taylor has built up the view that in the modern form of the ethic of authenticity, with the related processes of self-development and self-advancement – all orientated around subjectivism and individualism – is the given and the goal, albeit one that regularly falls into deviation. This cultural scenario presents the challenge as to whether it is possible to engage with this perspective rationally to reinstate the truer form of the ethic of authenticity.

Specifically, Taylor aims to make a coherent defence of

---

[1] As before – see *Sources* pp. 3-24: Chapter 1 of *Sources* is entitled 'Inescapable Frameworks'.

authentic self-development as he has so far defined it, whilst sustaining a critique of the deviant variant of 'soft relativism', this in a way that combats the countering view, the argument that the neutralism of soft relativism is a natural consequence and feature of human life; this in particular within social and cultural settings where moral subjectivism and individualism have come to bear. As we indicated earlier, this amounts to an alternative diagnosis to the pattern of development Taylor charts, to give the view that the tradition he favours naturally leads to narcissistic subjectivity and the morality of neutralism. Taylor's mission is to show how the truly authentic ethical ideal of authenticity is a rationally explicable alternative to this trend. If it is not over-labouring the point, one might say that this business is the major intellectual challenge Taylor faces in the text.

Taylor launches into his explanation with the claim that rational dialogue is only possible with those who are open to reason: 'Reasoning in moral matters is always reasoning with somebody' (p. 31). He says that we cannot reason 'from the ground up' (p. 32) as if you could argue with someone who did not accept any moral values whatsoever. It would be as impossible as trying to discuss 'empirical matters' with someone who 'refused to accept the world of perception around us'. The nub of the matter is whether it is possible to have rational discourse with 'people who are deeply into soft relativism, or who seem to accept no allegiance higher than their own self-development' (p. 31).

The capacity for rational discourse is, as Taylor appreciates, usually assumed to presuppose cogent language use, intellectual self-critical awareness, openness to self-criticism and objective self-assessment. For such reasons and as all parents know, rational discussion with two-year-olds, and indeed many teenagers, is often unfruitful. Rational discourse is as tricky with those of any age who hold to their ideas as a form of absolute and non-negotiable truth – although, in *Authenticity*, this alternative line in intractability is not one Taylor pursues. As to the criteria for rational discourse, rational views are those we hold or reject on the quality and weight of evidence, including the evidence of shared experience and coherent argument. Argument and evidence are uncontroversial parts of what we use as reasonable individuals, capable of self-consciously operating by reference to the rules of rational argument.

In a narrative of development from Descartes to Herder as considered in the previous section, Taylor thinks that self-critical reasoned selfhood emerged; this is still in evidence and is recoverable, but nevertheless, in modernity, reasoned self-critical thought and the ideal of authenticity have been diminished. Following Bloom's review, the problem we have seen Taylor attending to is that those who shape their lives according to the modern but debased version of the ideal of authenticity are doing so in the narrowed and flattened sense of individualised self-development.[1] The modern deviant version of the moral ideal of authenticity tends to resist rational demands for justification for the reasons we have seen, linking subjectivism, individuality and views related to egalitarian liberalism. People enjoy the idea that they are free to think and act as they please without inhibitions from others, with their self-affirmation a sufficient guarantor of the given choices. Again, it might be gender self-affirmation or one's preferences for this rather than that brand of chocolate; the subjective preference is considered self-justifying.

To counter this and consider the case for the true ideal of authenticity, we need, Taylor suggests, to ask 'two orders of questions' (p. 32) that 'interweave, or perhaps shade into each other'. These are: 'What are the conditions in human life of realizing an ideal of this kind?', and '… what does

---

[1] See above, Chapters 2 and 3.

the ideal properly understood call for?'

To develop these points, Taylor makes a positive move by developing, without using the phrase, a key aspect of what elsewhere he terms his 'moral ontology', by describing 'the general feature of human life' (p.32) that he wants to 'evoke' (p. 33): this is what he terms its *dialogical* character'.

The 'Dialogical' *Character of Life*

Taylor now draws on a fundamental assumption about life, and what it is to be human that is also grounded in the residual origins of academic life: we go back to Plato's determination to use interpersonal dialogues grounded in social relations of friendship to give exoteric expression to the intellectual matters he wanted to explore. One could say common sense confirms this, as well as strands in contemporary thought whereby the interpersonal socio-linguistic structures of cultural and social life are seen as preconditions for personal being.[1] The core idea here is that we become who we are and become so in a better way through our being with and association with others. Taylor's version of this idea is expressed with the view that to become 'full human agents' with self-understanding and a sense of self-identity, we have to acquire the 'rich human languages of expression'. Here Taylor – anticipating what he also says in the Kyoto Lecture we referenced earlier – takes 'language' in the wider sense, to include the expressive forms of verbal and written language, as well as the communicative forms of 'art', 'gesture', and 'love' (p. 33). The blindingly obvious point is that we do not acquire these languages in an isolated condition but in the crucible of family and group life. These groupings may at times be arduous and inhospitable, but the residual point is that we

---

[1] Wittgenstein's thought combines all of these elements in a distinctive fashion. I have written on this separately: see Loxton (2020), especially pp. 111-153.

acquire 'languages of expression' through a process of enculturing induction through dialogue with others who are prior.

Taylor gets support for this by referencing G. H. Mead's notion of 'significant others' to develop the view that the 'genesis of the human mind is not "monological", not something each accomplishes on his or her own, but dialogical'.[1] Taylor again stresses that this view does not preclude that humans can benefit from activities undertaken through 'solitary reflection'. Our own ideas and thoughts are often best clarified through this type of thinking. However, for 'the definition of our identity' and other such 'important issues', we work up our sense of things 'always in dialogue with, sometimes in struggle against, the identities our significant others want to recognize in us'. It is through 'exchanges with others who matter to us' that individuals gain the means to be self-developers, and this reveals that there is always a backdrop and point of reference for that individualisation, creativity, and for the capacity for rational thought.

Taylor's view is that we continue to operate in the tension of dialogue with others to express, explain, justify and orientate our self-perspectives. Thus personal self-development, our authentication properly understood, is always '*dialogical.*'

It is hard to underestimate the importance of this dialogic perspective to Taylor's project. As we know from his remarks in the first Section of *Authenticity*, he has grave

---

[1] G. H. Mead (1863-1931) – American philosopher, sociologist and psychologist. Mead spent most of his academic career at Chicago University. His main argument was that it was from social interaction that language arose and had significance. A model academic, Mead lectured and taught, and wrote notes and papers, but published nothing. After his death, his students published volumes of his writings. One of these was *Mind, Self and Society* (1934), and it is to this that Taylor refers (*Authenticity* p. 33 n. 24).

reservations about 'instrumental reason' (p. 5), and he is looking to reaffirm the human capacity for a non-instrumental form of reason to allow humanity to rise above narrow outlooks or prejudices, as in the ideal of the rational Enlightenment. Instrumental reason sets up a positive vibe due to its predilection for efficiency in delivering tangible benefits. However, this comes at a price, in terms of the 'ends that ought to be guiding our lives' being 'eclipsed by the demand to increase output'. Taylor sees amelioration through the use of 'disengaged rationality' (p. 25), which offers wider perspectives for critical and positive thought, but now a richer option comes through into the operational method of the defence and expression of authenticity. We see now that the preference is for a capacity for reasoning about issues of morality, which is always reasoning 'with somebody' (p. 31), based on his characterisation of human life as '*dialogical*' (p. 33). Here we have a form of what we might term interpersonal or relational reasoning.

Taylor thinks that some would want to maintain that self-authentication and self-definition thereby involve states or processes of association with others simply as a means to the end of authenticating the individual. However, for Taylor, this is the distorted model of the ethic of authenticity. He has a point: humans are not like paper aeroplanes: made, perhaps with great care, but then launched on what often proves to be a one-way solo flight. Again, humans are long in the processes of nurturing in social units, predominantly the family, and so gradually acquire the capacities to enter into wider relational and dialogic modes of life. Taylor moves to insist on the dialogical aspect as being central to the true ideal of authenticity. Community as a primary mode of being enables, through dialogue, many variant forms of self-fulfilment. The individual's potential for distinctive identity is maximally empowered by relationships and through shared, related forms of life. Here Taylor again implies a participative form of moral ontology for the human condition.[1]

Taylor employs the idea of the 'monological ideal' (p. 34) to indicate the view that is the emergent but distorted form of the ideal of authenticity, where what is held to is the sense of 'relationships' as necessary 'to fulfil but not to define ourselves'. This is a debased form of the ideal, evident in situations where people seek gratification from others for their own benefit rather than through a reciprocal relationship. This variant of the ideal of authenticity is below par because the 'dialogical' aspect of life is underestimated. 'Common enjoyment' is Taylor's example of what illuminates the added value given by dialogic experiences, the sharing of those things or experiences that come within the spectrum of 'the good things in life' with those 'we love'. From this, Taylor thinks that the formation of 'our identity' is hard to imagine without 'the people we love'. He concludes that these reciprocal dialogical relationships are 'the background' from which 'our tastes and desires and opinions and aspirations make sense'.

Dialogic life can, Taylor notes, be presented as restricting individual freedom and so as a form of inhibition over life. The 'hermit' (p. 35) or the 'solitary artist' are examples suggested of individual types who do not submit to relational dialogic life of the type highlighted by Taylor. However, both the hermit and the artist come from and seek an ongoing dialogic mode of being. The hermit might have God as 'interlocutor'; the solitary artist has the audience for whom he or she works.

Having introduced, defined and defended the dialogic character of life, Taylor provides the largest element so far in his positive doctrine of the ethic of authenticity. The concept he defends now presents self-authentication as an ethical ideal that relies upon relational dialogic associations

---

[1] On the wider issues here see Kerr (2004).

with others in a reciprocal mode of fulfilment. Within dialogic life comes, as mentioned, the 'disengaged rationality' (p. 25) that Taylor wants to use as a basis to show the contrasting inadequacy of the 'self-centred' and 'narcissistic' forms of contemporary aspiration for authenticity. Underlying all of the positive views here is, one feels, Taylor's 'ineradicable' sense of respect for persons.[1]

Horizons against Self-Centred and Narcissistic Forms of the Ideal

What Taylor wants to expose and reject are versions of the ideal of authenticity that propose self-fulfilment without (a) 'the demands of our ties to others' (p. 35) and (b) without the demands 'emanating from something more or other than human desires or aspirations'. This latter point attests to what happens if life is orientated to our own individualised projects of authentication. We are then manifesting what Taylor sees as the narcissistic deviations from the ideal of the ethics of authenticity. Taylor is clear that the trends represented by this false version of the ideal of authenticity are 'self-defeating'.

Taylor decides to consider the second trend (b), first, and in the margin of his text, at this point, we have the signifier '1)'.[2] We will look on through this section in vain for the '2)' to indicate where Taylor moves to discuss the first trend a): 'the demands of our ties to others' – for the 2) appears right at the start of the next section (p. 43). Perhaps this is a hangover from the text used for the Radio Talks being put together as the book manuscript with the section divisions being placed without checking where these other bits of notation lay.

Proceeding to discuss b), Taylor says that in respect of the

---

[1] See *Sources* p. 8.
[2] This is on p. 35 of the text.

'demands of authenticity itself as an ideal' (p. 35), if we try to define within ourselves what is original or distinctive 'we have to take as background some sense of what is significant'. He means that the sense a person might have of their distinctiveness comes from their relations with and differences from others, which of course, means that the sense we have of our distinct identity and worth is dependent on relational dialogic encounters with others.

Taylor reinforces these points with examples of activities that are self-authenticating, including that 'I define myself by my ability to articulate important truths' or by the ability 'to play the Hammerklavier like no one else' and to 'revive the traditions of my ancestors' (p. 36).[1] These activities are understood to 'have human significance'. The key idea is that in such activities, self-definition comes through the contrasts that can be found with how others do or have done these significant things. It is this 'domain of recognizable self-definitions' that gives the means for rejecting the pseudo-ideal of authenticity given by the soft-relativist subjectivist, who tries to maintain that an individual derives a distinct sense of authentic worth through self-defined personal feeling alone. Taylor does not think this 'an intelligible claim' – again, this is the narcissistic variant of the distorted ideal of authenticity. Personal feelings alone are never a sufficient warrant for a reasoned or justified sense of authenticity, and 'soft relativism self-destructs' (p. 37).

All this is for Taylor a subset of a more general theory of meaning and truth, to which we referred earlier, which is that the importance or significance of things is set against a 'background of intelligibility', which he likes to call a 'horizon' (p. 37).

---

[1] The 'Hammerklavier' here is a reference to Beethoven's Piano Sonata No. 29, Opus 106 – a work of formidable depth, range and difficulty.

As indicated earlier, with the references to 'horizons', Taylor is drawing on ideas from *Sources*, the first chapter of which is called 'Inescapable Frameworks'.[1] Within that earlier treatment, Taylor notes that the term 'horizon' can be used for the frameworks, which are defined as 'that in virtue of which we make sense of our lives spiritually. Not to have a framework is to fall into a life which is spiritually senseless'.[2]

From what Taylor has been saying, the realm of social interaction and dialogue with others might be one vital horizon, but the frameworks that are noted are those of the 'warrior and honour ethic' of classical Greece, traditional Christian religion and morality, and Platonic metaphysics.[3]

Given these instances, it would seem that with the 'spiritual' aspect of life that he is keen to make sense of, Taylor is not thinking of a narrowly religious sense of spiritual, but rather of a culturally rich version. Taylor also notes the challenges that come to the horizons, from Weber and Nietzsche, who uses the image of a horizon being wiped away in his famous 'Death of God' passage.[4] While Weber's thinking is also found in *Authenticity*, the review of Nietzsche is not carried over.

Taylor's thinking here is linked to some ideas he develops in *Sources*. His valuation of engaging individual life with the backdrop of frameworks or horizons relates to the insights of the continental phenomenologists, including Husserl and Merleau-Ponty. They, in distinct ways, shared a project to conduct 'the retrieval of the lived experience or creative activity underlying our awareness of the world,

---

[1] See *Sources* pp. 3-24 and Chapter 3 above.
[2] *Sources* p. 18.
[3] *Sources* p. 16f.
[4] We will consider this shortly.

which had been occluded or denatured by the regnant mechanist construal'.[1] This point is, in effect, a challenge to the deviant trends of instrumentalism, atomisation and fragmentation that Taylor reviews in *Authenticity*. In contrast, thinking about Taylor's development of the dialogic character of human life, he could have used the notion of a horizon explicitly within his portrayal of the 'dialogic' nature of relations earlier in the section since the relational boundary of others is a qualitative horizon for the identity and development of the individual.

However, what Taylor wants to stress is the view that as the deviant forms of the ideal of authenticity rest on subjectivism, they deny all significance to 'horizons': this is seen as self-defeating and self-contradictory.

In a telling phrase, Taylor says of horizons, that:

'… one of the things we can't do, if we are to define ourselves significantly, is suppress or deny the horizons against which things take on significance for us.'

We will return to this matter in a moment, but first, a type of commercial break. Two contrasting approaches to the issue of horizons can inform what we find with Taylor: from Nietzsche, we have one of the more dramatic assaults on the credibility of horizons and with John Donne, a meditative reflection on the vital importance of what we might term the life horizon of others.

---

[1] *Sources* p. 460. Edmund Husserl (1859-1938). German philosopher who was the founder of the phenomenological school of thought as developed by Heidegger, Merleau-Ponty and others. I am very grateful to Charles Taylor for confirming this school of thought as providing a basis for his thinking on horizons, this through by a brief email dialogue (14/09/21).

Interludes on Horizons from Nietzsche and Donne[1]

Here there is a case to make some allusions to offer commentary on the themes developed by the often highly allusive Taylor. For a reference to the idea of losing horizons, as we have just seen, the most powerful image would perhaps be Nietzsche's in *The Gay Science*, where we have the parabolic account of the madman who, in the bright light of noon, runs about the market place with a lantern, looking for God. As mentioned, Taylor refers to this passage in *Sources*, but he does not allude to it in *Authenticity*.[2]

In Nietzsche's parable, the madman is mocked by passers-by, many of whom do not believe in God:

'The madman jumped into their midst and pierced them with his eyes. "Whither is God?" he cried. "I will tell you. *We have killed him* – you and I. All of us are all his murderers. But how did we do this? How could we drink up the sea? Who gave us the sponge to wipe away the entire horizon? What were we doing when we unchained this earth from its sun? Whither is it moving now? Whither are we moving now? Away from all suns? Are we not plunging continually? Backward, sideward, forward, in all directions? Is there still any up or down? Are we not straying as through an infinite nothing? Do we not feel the breath of empty space? Has it not become colder? Is not night continually closing in on us? Do we not need to light lanterns in the morning? Do we not hear anything yet of the noise of the gravediggers who are burying God? Do we smell nothing as yet of the divine decomposition? Gods, too, decompose. God is dead. God remains dead. And we have killed him. How shall we comfort ourselves,

---

[1] On the matter of horizons, Isaiah Berlin sometimes refers to the 'human horizon'. This has been explained as an idea used to express the sense of 'a fence which encloses both our basic shared values and a wide variety of other possible values that are recognizably human but not universally subscribed to.' Hardy (2018) p. 180. For more on Berlin's view see Hardy (2018) pp. 180f and pp. 236ff.
[2] See *Sources* p. 17.

the murderers of all murderers? What was holiest and mightiest of all that the world has yet owned has bled to death under our knives: who will wipe this blood off us? What water is there for us to clean ourselves? What festivals of atonement, what sacred games shall we have to invent? Is not the greatness of this deed too great for us? Must we ourselves not become gods simply to seem worthy of it?"[1]

The madman fails to move the crowd, and so in despair, he appreciates that he has 'come too early'. News of the event of the death of God – meaning the death of the idea of God and all absolutes – has yet to reach the ears of the people. And this is a view that Nietzsche shares with his madman.

The passage from Nietzsche is significant for the use, akin to Taylor's, of the image of the horizon. Whereas Taylor wants us to recognise the 'background of intelligibility' he terms 'a horizon', Nietzsche is the great obliterator of all such horizons. As we see in Nietzsche's parable, the horizon is 'sponged away' – not the literal horizon – but those of meaning and value that are taken to render experience intelligible. Nietzsche' point is that this horizon is a fiction, and the madman has in effect exposed an alternative reality, a world devoid of meaning, inhabited by people living in an artificial scheme of outmoded values. Nietzsche's view implies that humanity, and so culture, has misunderstood the rise of critical thought, the age of the Enlightenment, romanticism and the modern age in general, and Taylor agrees up to a point with this diagnosis, in that the ideal, and the advent of the distorted ideal of authenticity, emerge and develop through this period. Nietzsche's parabolic narrative gives an evocative vision of how reality is when we grasp the consequences of contingency and relativity without the active re-valuing of life by individuals, from whom alone, he thinks, values, truths and meanings can be created.

---

[1] Nietzsche (1974): 125. I say more about this in my study of Nietzsche – see Loxton (2021), especially Chapter 6.

According to Nietzsche's madman, our progress in thought at one level has wiped away 'the entire horizon'. As this is a parabolic passage, we must stress that the horizon in question is not the physical one but all that is entailed by intellectual and cultural parameters for meaning and truth. All forms of realism and certainty as hitherto taken as read are removed – and in the parabolic narrative, the tragic comedy lies in this not being appreciated by the townsfolk who live as if they can still order their lives around some version of custom and belief. In this, Nietzsche is determinedly operating 'monologically', as Taylor puts it, placing all the emphasis for a recovery of values on the endeavours of heroic individuals and doing without the 'horizons of significance' that Taylor affirms.

On the core issue of whether we can defend coherent 'horizons', there is much dispute to be had.[1] In common characterisations, either we have 'horizons', as in classical reason, for example, or you have none, as in Nietzsche, and in other variant idioms of relativism and subjectivism. However, what Taylor proposes is, to restate his case, that 'to define ourselves, to determine in what our originality consists, we see that we have to take as background some sense of what is significant' (p. 35). This entails the 'horizons against which things take on significance for us' (p. 37). Taylor adds this to his characterisation of the human condition involving dialogic, relational associations as a vital element in the ethical restorative for modernity. Is this a viable project of restoration, or is Taylor trying to square the circle?

As an example of the issues as he sees them, Taylor turns to the debate over sexual orientation and the case that some make that there can be no exclusive standard of appropriate sexual orientation: sexual orientation, it can be argued, is a

---

[1] Again, for more on this in relation to Nietzsche's thought see Loxton (2021). I argue there that Nietzsche does not actually support subjectivism or relativism.

matter of self-determination, a matter of personal choice, a matter for self-defining freedom.[1] With this perspective, as it is usually expressed in modernity, the view emerges that there is no normality. Hence, all options 'are equally worthy', all are 'freely chosen, and it is choice that confirms worth' (p. 37). This sounds akin to the scenario suggested by Nietzsche's madman: on this view, there could be no 'horizon of meaning' for sexual orientation, no sense of pre-existing standards of worth or value.

Taylor thinks there are matters where personal choice or taste is crucial. In personal relationships, whether someone prefers a 'taller or shorter' sexual partner or whether someone prefers 'blondes or brunettes' (p. 38) is a matter of personal choice. In contrast, choices over sexual orientation make sense only against a background with 'the existence of a pre-existing horizon of significance, whereby some things are worthwhile and some things less so, and still others not at all, quite anterior to choice'. If we allow choices over sexual orientation to be made as a matter of self-affirmation, Taylor thinks that this means that the 'choice of sexual orientation loses any special significance'.

Taylor's point suggests that such a view represents the triumph of image over substance, fancy over virtue, and mere want over rational need. Would, we could ask, such a *laissez-faire* approach hold good in medicine? In teaching? In parenting? In legal advice? In any matters that matter?

Taylor makes many allusions and references in *Authenticity* his book, but he does not cite John Donne, but Donne's fourteenth 'Meditation' contains lines that resonate with the dialogic issues raised by Taylor.[2] Reflecting on the tolling

---

[1] See *Authenticity* pp. 37-38.
[2] Taylor does not refer to Donne in *Sources*. John Donne (1572-1631). Donne is now best known for his poems and meditative writings. He became an Anglican priest and duly Dean of St Pauls. In his youth he was a venturer, a soldier and man of the world.

church bell that was summoning him to attend a funeral service, the poet realises that the bell is a summons, not just to commemorate the life that has just passed, it is a call to him and indeed, to all, for all lose from the death and passing of anyone. It is a reminder that the actions of the Church – the people writ large – is of concern to all, an inescapable horizon providing orientation for those who envision it. As Donne puts it:

'No man is an island, entire of itself; every man is a piece of the continent, a part of the main. If a clod be washed away by the sea, Europe is the less, as well as if a promontory were, as well as if a manor of thy friend's or of thine own were. Any man's death diminishes me, because I am involved in mankind; and therefore never send to know for whom the bell tolls; it tolls for thee'.[1]

Donne's insight that 'I am involved in mankind' travels deeply into Taylor's dialogic domain of interest, for recharging the individual's self-understanding is grounded in the significance gained through associative relations with others, through being a part of the greater whole of humankind. This has a clear affinity with Taylor's moral ontology of interpersonalism, his notion of the '*dialogical*' (p. 33), and his view of 'our identity being formed by the people we love' (p. 34). It links too with the notion he develops in *Sources* that human morality can only make sense if individuals operate in a setting of 'moral space.'[2] This entails the sense of 'contact', meaning the sense of a relationship 'incorporating something in one's life or connecting to something greater outside.'[3] These are crucial, generic aspects of life, which combine to give another point where Taylor's 'respect for persons' thesis seems close to hand. They provide a restorative to the otherwise over-individualised deviant form of the ideal of

---

[1] Donne (1959) pp. 107-108.
[2] See *Sources* pp. 25-52.
[3] *Sources* p. 44.

authenticity.[1]

Taylor needs some aid to give his restorative efficacy. Without it, he faces a potential two-aspect problem, with a logical and ethical character: he wants to say that the ethic of authenticity has to do with the individual's chosen pattern of self-development; yet this choice cannot be wholly free and autonomous, for it has to have validation through dialogue with 'horizons of significance'. This stipulation seems to qualify freedom. As a reviewer of Taylor's book put it, it is not at all clear how this referential relation to the 'horizons of significance' is anything other than a 'threat to freedom'.[2]

As Taylor presents it, a person is truly free within the associations they have with the 'horizons of significance'. In effect, we are truly free only if we have genuine choices, and this is how Taylor sees the scenario with the relationship we have to the horizons. This association is one thing, but it seems to assume the status and ethical value of the 'horizons of significance'. By what means can we establish and then know the worth of these 'horizons' of significance? Would we not need to know independently by some other criteria that a putative 'horizon' was actual, and ethically sound? If not, the questions arise about how the appeal to 'horizons' is anything more than purely rhetorical? If, however, 'horizons' could include the dynamics of the dialogic domain of interpersonal life, why not say so clearly?

Taylor's move is to take another shot at the nature of recent conventions, and, as in his example of issues of sexual orientation, he says that what that entails is that everything

---

[1] See *Sources* p. 8.
[2] 1993 Review of Charles Taylor's *Ethics of Authenticity* by David McCabe – online at
https://indexarticles.com/reference/commonweal/the-ethics-of-authenticity/

is considered to be a matter of personal choice. The prevailing view, and of course, the deviant version of the ideal, entails that there is a range of factors, highly particularised, that cannot be a part of 'discriminating judgements', because it is in the end, dependent 'on how you feel' (p. 38). In much more recent times, the issue of gender assignation, to which we referred earlier, involving the view that a person can choose and affirm their gender assignation for themselves as a matter of personal choice, has been prevalent and highly controversial, not least for the reasons Taylor gives in respect of sexual orientation.[1]

Taylor's view is that in all such matters, what is seen as the deviant form of authenticity legitimises self-affirmed choices disconnected from references to the values based on moral horizons. To Taylor, this is to affirm the self in a situation without engaging the crucial notions of identity, personhood, respect and equality. For Taylor, personal choices have a real moral sense if they are orientated to horizons of meaning that shape the context for informed decisions.

The idea emerging is that to recapture an ethically sound approach, authenticating choices over, for example, homosexual as opposed to heterosexual commitments, this should be made against a background – or horizon – of real sexual experiences, within life and through thought, and to aid us in seeing how Taylor thinks this can work, we pick up on what seems to be his key redemptive point what, drawing on imagery from the impeccable source of Clint Eastwood westerns, we might term Taylor's 'the Good, the Bad and the Ugly' point about 'horizons'. He observes that with reference to 'a prexisting horizon of significance', the practical issue is that what can be found and tested out from this are options that are 'worthwhile' in contrast with 'others' that are 'less so, and still others not at all'.

---

[1] On gender orientation and the issues arising see Joyce (2021).

From this, we see that the horizons are, therefore, and helpfully, suddenly akin to a market: just as in a market we can shop around, and find goods and wares that are past their shelf-life, worn out, shoddy – or in great condition and fit for use, so we can investigate and try out the options for life and welfare within the spectrum of the 'horizons of significance'. This means that the 'horizons' are not undifferentiated and to be followed as if they were directly prescriptive. As with the market analogy, it is more a case of using reasoned judgment to find pathways, perspectives and patterns, giving the best options for life from whatever is within the mix.

From the presentation so far, we do this drawing on disengaged rationality, our creative individuality and the process of dialogic relations. Against Nietzsche and against over-prescriptive measures, the 'general lesson is that authenticity can't be defended in ways that collapse horizons of significance' (pp. 38-39).

Taylor's Emergent Proposals

In developing his emerging view, Taylor maintains that we must defend the ethical ideal, keeping intact the 'horizons of significance'. The key reason for this is that the sense of life having meaning and worth comes from its being chosen. Furthermore, the implication is that it is chosen from and in relation to the spectrum of insights and options set within the 'horizon of significance'. This is how Taylor sees the core truth of what is meant by self-defining and self-determining freedom. This freedom 'depends on the understanding that *independent of my will*, there is something noble, courageous, and hence significant, in giving shape to my own life' (p. 39).

With reference to the 'something noble, courageous, and... significant', we have a clear sense of a background or substratum of something that operates as a given, a source, root or ideal of value. Just as a market exists and operates independent of my will, so do horizons of significance operate. The connotations of nobility and courage Taylor mentions suggest the values embodied in the tradition of virtue thinking, Enlightenment ideals such as the imperative charge for individuals to have 'the courage to use your own reason', and aspects of Nietzsche's neo-classical revivalism.[1] This raises an important question as to whether the ethic of authenticity is only viable for those who have moved through a classical to the enlightenment intellectual and cultural tradition. If so, it becomes unclear how the ethic of authenticity can emerge for the developing world. It also provokes the sense that for all Taylor's concerns to shape an ideal of authenticity related to the human capacity to be individually true to themselves, the inescapable horizons are, we recall, 'pre-existing horizons of significance' (p. 38). The real point is that the choices that an individual makes to give shape to their life are set against important issues within and for that life, but, says Taylor, 'which issues are significant *I* do not determine. If I did, no issue would be significant… then the very ideal of self-choosing *as a moral ideal* would be impossible (p. 39).

What is clear is that Taylor wants to hold to the notion that there are valid 'horizons of significance', which are the true and legitimate means of correlation for the drive for self-creation. The breadth of resources within the 'horizons' empowers choices that lead to authentic decision-making, and without that backdrop of meaning, the ideal of authenticity is distorted because 'the ideal of self-choice supposes that there are other issues of significance beyond self-choice'. Developing his view, Taylor refers to aspects of J. S. Mill's argument on this theme in *On Liberty*; referring to Mill's case for individuals to choose for themselves their mode of life: Taylor wants to reaffirm that

---

[1] See, for example, Nietzsche (1998) Sections 257-296 & Nietzsche (2008) Essay 1: 16-17; Essay 2: 20-24. This topic is discussed further in Loxton (2021) Chapter 1.

such choosing is trivial and incoherent if it is validated merely by the act of choice. The ethical ideal of authenticity is again affirmed as deriving its validity from the fact that some choices are better than others, that choices, including better ones, are made from a background horizon of meaning, and that self-defining freedom as an ethical ideal has to be more than a subjective preference; there has to be engagement with others, and this returns us to the dialogical or relational view as outlined earlier in the section.[1]

Taylor then has another reference, this time connecting with Nietzsche and his project of re-writing the 'table of values' (p. 40) – what Nietzsche termed the business of 'revaluing all values'.[2] This fine-sounding phrase amounts to the capacity humans have to reverse the pattern and shape of their values. Taylor sees this as a valid project in principle, but he thinks it only works if it focuses on redefining values concerning 'important questions'. A purely arbitrary self-creation through choice is of no more worth than choosing what to wear or what to select from the menu at some fast-food outlet. Warming to his theme, Taylor says that self-creation cannot exclude 'history' or 'the bonds of solidarity' – another version of the 'ties of others'. Arbitrary self-choosing is again characterised as that which 'flattens and narrows' the self. Against this, the conditions of significance for authentic selfhood are explicit: 'I can define my identity only against the background of things that matter'. The candidates for what matters cannot be ignored or ruled out. Again, Taylor sets out his view directly:

'Only if I exist in a world in which history, or the demands of nature, or the duties of citizenship, or the needs of my fellow human beings, or the call of God, or something else of this order *matters* crucially, can I define an identity for myself that is not trivial. Authenticity is not the enemy of demands that emanate

---

[1] For Mill on choosing the way to live see Mill (1987), especially Chapter 3.
[2] On this Loxton (2021), especially Chapter 16.

from beyond the self; it supposes such demands' (p. 40-41).

Here we should log the given instances of the now clearer 'inescapable horizons': we have 'history', the 'demands of nature', the 'duties of citizenship', the 'needs of one's fellow humans', the 'call of God'. A point that arises from this outline of horizons is that we have the generalised reference to 'history', the very contemporary as well as classical and theological 'demands of nature', the political and moral 'duties' and 'needs', and the theological and metaphysical 'call of God'. Given the approach that Taylor has in his book, as well as in his writing in general, what he has in mind with history and the moral and political dimensions of life, including environmentalism, is reasonably clear. How and whether these must correlate with equally inescapable theological or religious horizons is more controversial. That Taylor says 'or something else of this order' suggests he is not being over-prescriptive in his horizontal aspirations. What matters is that 'something of this order *matters* crucially'. He is on the track of saying, as Donne suggests, that no one is like an isolated and self-sufficient Island: we are all a part of a geography of life, a narrative, a background, a culture and a history, with ideals and values that can shape and make us through the amalgam of our intuitive and rational choices.

However, it seems from Taylor's defence of the active ideal of authenticity that individuals have to freely orientate to some value from this background of horizons to achieve the ethical ideal of authenticity and so to avoid triviality. His view is that it is only through wrestling with this that we define and appreciate how we are different or distinctive.

The long and the short of what Taylor offers with the ethical ideal of authenticity is that an appeal is made to the macro patterns within the cultural and historical tradition rather than a micro-theoretical scheme of thought honed and polished by critical reason. In relation to the 'horizons of significance', found within and as vital parts of the background narrative of culture, history and life, we as individuals, but through dialogic associations, make authentic choices to make our lives our own.

Taylor's scheme now assumes shape and form, with some clearer hints on content. We have considered the problem that if we are to derive our sense of values from the pre-existent horizons of moral significance, this raises the question as to how we evaluate the worth of these horizons sufficient to notice and assess. Taylor's sense of the plurality of values within the horizons helps us see how we resource a critical insight to enable the assessment that avoids the snares of the debased forms of the ideal.[1]

Taylor's dialogic model helps solve this in that his idea is that our lives radiate outward into the lives of others. We grow through our associations and so find ourselves embedded in the organic of dialogic life. This is how we find resonant values in the inescapable horizons of family, friendship, within areas of education and work, in the patterns of culture and reflection that, if we are lucky, hover around us. Here, if all is well, we grow the skill, the depth of feeling and the powers of reason to become authentic individuals allied to the ideal in Taylor's understanding. A problem with this model is that no one gets to choose the life they have or the horizons that surround them. There would be one set of dialogic associations and horizons of intelligibility in Canada, but a rather different set if we radiated out from a life in, say, Afghanistan. Riding our luck or good fortune is, perhaps, another skill to acquire.

---

[1] For more on value pluralism see Berlin (2017) p. x, pp. 212-217 and for more discussion of this see Hardy (2018) pp. 183-261.

Reading/Revision Questions **Section IV**: *Inescapable Horizons*

Makes notes to define, illustrate and explain the following:

1. Why does Taylor think there could be a problem reasoning with people who 'are immersed in the contemporary culture of authenticity'.

2. What is the importance to Taylor of the 'dialogical' character of human life?

3. What does Taylor take from the work of G. H. Mead?

4. Explain the importance to Taylor of distinguishing 'monological' and 'dialogical' understandings of the human condition.

5. Why does no one acquire the languages needed for self-definition on his or her own?

6. How does Taylor link love and identity?

7. Why does Taylor think that the more self-centred modes of contemporary culture are 'manifestly inadequate'?

8. Why does Taylor think that soft relativism self-destructs?

9. How does Taylor explain his idea of 'a background of intelligibility'?

10. What does Taylor do to show that we need to relate self-determining freedom to something '*independent*' of the will?

11. How does Taylor use J. S. Mill and Nietzsche to develop his defence of choice and 'horizons of importance'?

12. What do we learn about Taylor's idea of defining our identity in the last two pages of the section?

6. On 'The Need for Recognition' – Section V

Personal and Instrumental Problems

At the opening of this section, we see in the margin at the '2)' that is a hangover from the orientation of points for review in the previous section. Now the issue, to do with 'the demands of our ties with others' (p. 35), is taken up, under this section's title, 'The Need for Recognition'.

Taylor has given some form and content to his developing exposition of *The Ethics of Authenticity*, focusing on dialogic human relationships. He now wants to consider the matter left from the previous section of how self-fulfilment can be regarded as self-defeating when it involves a denial of commitment to others.

The issues at stake are to do with why the so-called debased form of the ideal of authenticity comes about and is so flawed. Working on this is, in a strong sense, another strand of the assault on what Taylor sees as the damaged version of the ideal of authenticity that he seeks to correct rather than to reject. His ability to make a convincing case over this matter is another major step in successfully building up the success of the positive restorative of authenticity that he affirms.

Taylor's focus is on the issue as to whether it is possible to sustain a view that says that we acquire our authentic self through quests for fulfilment that are 'purely personal' (p. 43). The 'contemporary culture of authenticity' is seen to affirm this and the consequent state, whereby for each person, their concerns, interests and associations are 'purely instrumental in their significance,' a trend that could be the real and inescapable outcome from the process of self-fulfilment. However, for Taylor, this would be the distorted model of the ideal of authenticity, the sense of individualism 'of anomie and breakdown' (p. 44), with 'no social ethic' but with the implication that all of the external relations a person has are simply means to the end of that person's self-fulfilment. This version of individualism is set against individualism 'as a moral principle or ideal (p. 45), which promotes 'some view on how the individual should live with others'. As should be clear from the previous section, life in the self-orientated mode of individualism means living without regard for a number of variant horizons, including history and culture, and with instrumental views of the community and towards commitments to political engagement, and sets up a highly marginal relation to others. At a personal level, it implies that interpersonal relationships are significant if, but only if, they are means to the end of the individual whose relationships they are.[1] This implies what can be termed, following Buber, an 'I-It' relation or 'subject-object' instrumentalism regarding others.[2] A relationship is 'secondary to the self-realisation of the partners' (p. 43).

An implication of this view is, for example, that no sort of reciprocal commitment, nor one that is selfless, makes sense unless it happens to coincide with self-orientated self-fulfilment. What cannot be entailed is any kind of longer-term reciprocal obligation, such as that of a life-long relational commitment. Taylor illustrates the trend he opposes using a quotation from another popular book of the period, Gail Sheehy's *Passages: Predictable Crises of Adult Life*.[3] This suggests that a key movement in life comes as individuals move away 'from institutional claims' and the agendas driven by 'other people'. In place of 'external valuations and accreditations', people move 'out of roles and into the self'. This sound like growing up and gaining

---

[1] It is like the scenario of fair-weather 'friends', 'friends' who are keen and eager when what you are or can offer is of use to them.

[2] See Buber (2000) on 'I-It' and 'I-Thou' relationships.

[3] Sheehy (1976). Gail Sheehy (1936-2020) – American author and journalist. Taylor (p. 44) quotes from p. 364 and p. 513 of Sheehy's book.

maturity through independence. It allows each individual:

'... to emerge reborn, *authentically* unique, with an enlarged capacity to love ourselves and embrace others… The delights of self-discovery are always available. Though loved ones move in and out of our lives, the capacity to love remains' (p. 44).

Taylor sees this affirmation of individual freedom as over-centred on the self in a way that 'distances us from our relations to others'. This is all expressive of the implausible distortion of the ideal ethic of authenticity against which Taylor wants to move towards a reconstruction of the ideal with the suggestion that the true 'ideal of authenticity incorporates some notions of society' and a sense of how 'people ought to live together'. In this part of his text, Taylor sounds again, rather Kantian, with his references to the obligations related to interpersonal dialogic modes of life, where we feel an imperative or two lurking in the background.

Taylor reinforces the view that the ideal ethic of authenticity entails creative individualism as in the modern sense, but also the view that to be an individual presupposes a social reality. The important thing is to work so as to distinguish myopic self-interested individualism with its propensity for subjectivism and weak relativism from individualism orientated to the horizon of responsive and responsible social intercourse. Picking up the theme of the book's opening, Taylor appeals to the great tradition of individual liberalism in modern thought. He specifically refers to Locke and the theme of individuals bonded through the social contract of consent; he alludes to 'later forms' of the 'great individualist philosophies – and perhaps means, or ought to mean, J. S. Mill and the sovereignty of the individual, related in Mill's view, to the principle of utility in 'the largest sense', related to the 'permanent interests of man as a progressive being'.[1]

Two Forms of Distortion to the Ideal of Authenticity

Taylor reasons that the culture of self-fulfilment that he opposes, which he sees as a distortion of the true ideal of authenticity, has two characteristic 'modes of social existence' (p. 45). The first is based on something we have already encountered, the emergent 'notion of universal right', meaning, he thinks, the principle of everyone having 'the right and capacity to be themselves'.

The doctrine of universal human rights, as in the UN Declaration, is one of the most highly valued and most often referenced notions of modernity, to the point that for many readers, as we noted earlier, it must be a shocking and near heretical challenge to encounter Taylor's claim that the notion 'underlies soft relativism', the ethos that says that 'no one has a right to criticize another's values'. With the view that the right of free choice is a part of the doctrine of universal human rights, the idea that one cannot seriously criticise what another has freely chosen becomes reciprocal. Taylor thinks this leads to an inclination for 'conceptions of procedural justice', meaning the habitual resort to the law to defend the equality of rights and opportunities for 'self-fulfilment'. There is limited justice in this approach for Taylor because it is grounded in an artificial, over-individualised sense of the human condition.

The second 'mode' involves a particular emphasis on personal relationships as the context for self-discovery and

---

[1] Mill (1987) pp. 69-70. The point is that here, Mill notably develops the notion of utility into something far more dynamic than the presentation his father James Mill (1773-1836), or Jeremy Bentham (1748-1832) had formally given. Mill's work to this end is evident in his writings on 'The Art of Life' in *A System of Logic* (1843). This is something I will examine in my forthcoming study of Mill, *Proper Guardians*.

authentic being. Sexual relationships are the particular focus for self-discovery and self-fulfilment, with one's sexual identity and sexual self-fulfilment being the ideal to be realised as the end by these means. This implies that the relationship is subordinate to the individual's self-related end. This, Taylor thinks, is a part of a trend that focuses on what is considered good in the everyday business of relational life. However, this does entail that personal fulfilment and identity 'requires recognition by others'. The 'ties to others' are not for unpicking.

Taylor thinks that this pair of trends have come about because of two changes that he notes and reviews. The first of these is what he terms the 'collapse of social hierarchies' (p. 46), whereby the ways of honouring individuals were placed in a system of hierarchical preferences. This meant that by default, only a very small percentage of people were honoured. In modern societies, honours in terms of the system for public awards (whether in Canada or the UK) retain something of this, the idea being that if everyone automatically became a Companion of Honour (CH), then the award would become meaningless.

Taylor's sense of a second change contrasts with the first point, as just explained, with the development of modern egalitarian notions of the essential worth and dignity of all humans. This is an ideal consistent with democratic values. However, the effect of this view is that with the 'inherent "dignity of human beings", or citizen dignity', we have an operational system of equalised worth and honour.

Politically, Taylor knows that equality is a powerful trend, but the upshot is that the concept of authentication becomes individualised and equalised. It becomes a very centred form of anthropocentrism, and individualism as a focus for the manifestation of equality becomes an end in itself to which all other orders are means. What happens is that the generalised pressure of equality operates to regulate and shape individuality.

Taylor's point is that while the ideal of the ethic of authenticity requires an act of 'inwardly generated identity' (p. 49) by the individual, this cannot be qualitatively or operationally effective in isolation: an individual's unique identity comes through 'open dialogue'. Taylor's reasoning on the structures within which we create languages of expression in the previous section – (p. 33) – and on creativity in performance – (p. 36) – are relevant to this point, as the following example shows:

If a concert pianist masters Shostakovich's 24 Preludes and Fugues Op. 87, she will not be at all happy just playing them to herself at home or in a closed arena to no one at all. Covid19 ground rules notwithstanding, the pianist wants to perform the work to an audience, whether live or through the media – or both. She wants her reading of the work, her interpretation, to be communicated interactively to others through the dialogical reality of attentive performance, for her interpretation to stand against previous performances, and through the reactions and responses, she hopes to show the worth and inspiration of the work and develop her distinct identity as a performer, an artist and a person.

We thus return through the circles of artistic commitment and appreciation to the concept of dialogic encounter. It is in and through the closest personal and expressive relationships that we have with significant others that we can progress in the authentic ideal of ethical self-making.

Explaining this theme, Taylor takes the view that the history and developing culture of authenticity has promoted and supported two distinct forms of living together. In the social context, there is an ethic of equality as 'fairness' (p. 50), with the principle of equality of opportunity for all to have the entitlement to be as they are and do so without prejudice over gender, sexual orientation, race and culture. Then, the 'identity-forming love-relationship' is seen as the primary mode of self-development and recognition.

Taylor entertains an apparent paradox: the spirit of the modern culture of authenticity suggests that all of an individual's relations are an instrumental means to the end of her authentic fulfilment. However, is this end alone consistent with the true ideal of authenticity? We already know that Taylor's answer to this will be 'No!'

Social and Personal Reconsiderations

Taylor approaches the problem in a measured way, looking again at both the social and personal aspects.

At the social level, Taylor explains that a case that might get wide support is that of thinking that self-orientated and instrumental forms of the ideal of authenticity could work within the framework of a system of 'procedural justice' (p. 51). This would give a strong defence to the rights of individuals to be equally different and cement an outlook of toleration. Taylor ponders this for a split second before saying that he does not think this, the basis for the previously discussed 'liberalism of neutrality', is a sufficient rationale for the ideal.

Taylor's point is that he does not think we can use a principle of toleration that amounts to allowing anything, however varied and diffuse. This turns the notion of equality into a kind of blanket for regulative sameness. Against this, we have to generate a sense of 'truly recognizing difference' so that the social principles of equality of regard can be related to some way of 'recognizing the equal value of different ways of being'. That people make different choices 'doesn't make them equal.' To properly ground equality of value, Taylor thinks that we need to recover a more robust method.

Taking a core example, he says that if 'men and woman are equal, it is not because they are different, but because overriding the difference are some properties, common or complementary, which are of value'. That people are 'capable of reason, or love, or memory, or dialogical recognition' suggests something of value that is 'common and complimentary'. So the argument is that any concept of equality has logically and as a matter of fact to be based on something shared: 'There must be some substantive agreement on value, or else the formal principle of equality will be empty and a sham' (p. 52). The idea of 'equal recognition' is empty unless 'we share something more'. Recognition presupposes difference, and recognising difference, 'like self-choosing, requires a horizon of significance, in this case, a shared one'.

Again there is an appeal to a 'horizon of significance' in terms of value, and with the emphasis on the capacity for responsive and responsible self-choosing, but in the context of a 'shared' area, we have the social and cultural settings for life that form parts of the background structure of 'inescapable horizons'. That human development is linked to participation in communal settings and against pre-existing background horizons of meaning still hints of an appeal to aspects of both Kantian and virtue thinking, but as we can now see, Taylor's radiant view of dialogic relations trumps these other, and he thinks, narrower ethical schemes.

On the personal side, Taylor considers the matter of human relationships, the view that instrumental thinking should be pervasive for this crucial aspect of life, giving a 'means to the end of self-fulfilment' rationale for the individual's relationships to others, is not, as we know, Taylor's view. He reaffirms that the truth about being human is that it is in the bonds of a loving relationship that we complete our development in what, in a moment of Aristotelian perspective, he terms a 'whole life' (p. 53).[1] Defining one's identity is to place it in a web of relations and commitments, to be dialogic and relational. If self-authentication is presented as what we find through assorted relations seen as means to that end, then self-authentication is at best a form of enjoyment that would, in the end, become 'self-stultifying'. However, if the end is what is found through dialogic encounters, then the true ideal of authenticity is enacted.

Taylor hopes that in his review so far, he has shown reasoned support for the restorable ideal of authenticity. However, to be sure this is the case, he wants to examine in closer detail the problem of subjectivism.

Reading/Revision Questions Section V*: The Need for Recognition.*

Makes notes to define, illustrate and explain the following:

1. At the start of the Section, Taylor looks at the 'personal understanding of self-fulfilment' and references ideas from a book by Gail Sheehy. What problems does he identify with this approach to human life?

2. How does Taylor show that authenticity entails a social side?

---

[1] Despite Taylor's rejection of the virtue tradition, here we have a clear echo of Aristotle's teaching on the life-long business of acquiring virtue: 'One swallow does not make a summer; neither does one day. Similarly, neither can one day, or a brief space of time, make a man blessed and happy.' Aristotle (2004) 1. 1098a 19-20.

3. What ideas come from Taylor's reference to Locke's individualism?

4. How does Taylor develop the case for seeing 'recognition by others' as important for self-fulfilment?

5. What two changes have led to 'modern preoccupation's with identity and recognition'?

6. What does Taylor think that issues of social recognition were not a problem in the past?

7. Why are intimate personal (or 'love') relationships seen as the 'crucibles of inwardly generated identity'?

8. Consider and assess what Taylor says in this Section about equality and fairness.

9. Why must there be substantive agreement on value so that the formal principle of equality does not become empty and a 'sham'?

10. What ideas emerge from this section about the form of authenticity as an ethical ideal?

7. On 'The Slide to Subjectivism' – Section VI

Sources of Deviation in the Ideal of Authenticity

We come to one of the longer sections of Taylor's book. The title is taken from a part of *Sources of the Self*, where 'a slide to subjectivism' as well as an 'anti-subjectivist thrust' is said to create a tension in the artistic and cultural mix of the early twentieth century.[1]

In *Authenticity's* version of this subjectivist slide, Taylor again puts his attention on the matter of how and why the ideal of the ethic of authenticity can fall into what he regards as the self-defeating perspective of subjectivism. To put it another way, how is it that a significant part of the culture of authenticity escaped the 'inescapable horizons'?

The review starts with a reminder of how we have been exploring variations on what is again (following Lasch) termed the modern 'culture of narcissism' (p. 55). On this variation from the ideal, self-fulfilment is seen as the true goal of life, but in a self-related individualistic manner and so to the exclusion of wider moral and social obligations. The clarification is given that self-related trends in authenticity are to be regarded as 'deviant' and 'trivialized'.

Taylor once more operates by saying that on this narcissistic culture, two perspectives can be taken; these he lists as (a) and (b) in the text. The first perspective (a) sees self-fulfilment as an ideal, as one that is as 'self-centred as the practices that flow from it' (p. 56). The second (b) sees self-fulfilment as self-indulgent egoism. Taylor then suggests that these two lines of thought tend to merge into one, as both diagnose self-indulgence as a core feature. Still, Taylor likes the distinction between the two because it allows him to characterize the alternative positions from which the

---

[1] See *Sources* p. 456.

perspectives come.

Taking a) into consideration, if we reach the view that self-fulfilment and its practices are fundamentally self-centred, we may think that morality is independent of reason or that self-fulfilment has nothing to do with relational or dialogic matters. It might be that this view is taken 'because one thinks of authenticity itself as a very low ideal, a rather thinly disguised appeal to self-indulgence'. Alternatively, 'because whatever the nature of contemporary ideals, one holds to a subjectivist view of moral convictions as mere projections that reason cannot alter'. Both strands of narcissism – a) and b) – are seen as being 'quite at peace' because the organisation of narcissism means that 'it is exactly in theory what it is in practice' and in its state of self-containment, it is 'impervious to argument'. If this were so, it would not be much of a help in the task of seeking a remedy. However, Taylor does not share this diagnosis of the culture of narcissism. He sees the culture as exhibiting 'tension' and 'to be living an ideal that is not fully comprehended'. His plan is that if he can draw out a fuller comprehension of the ideal of authenticity, this will 'challenge' the deviant practices and remind those living in the lesser form of the ideal that they share 'our human condition' and can be shown how 'these practices' – those of narcissism – are 'questionable' (pp. 56-57):

'The culture of narcissism lives an ideal that is systematically falling below' (p. 57).

Accordingly, Taylor wants to contrast these perspectives with his sense of the true ideal of an ethic of authenticity while exploring in more detail the reasons why the ideal is prone to the subjectivist deviation. Given that he has to show that this is a deviation and not the straight outcome of the ideal of being to one's own self true, this is, as we have said, a critical line of discussion within the project of retrieval.

144

Taylor begins by considering how the focus in modern life on having and fulfilling personal goals creates conflict with relational matters such as a person's wider obligations or commitments to others. The 'career versus family' tension is a classic example. Other examples would be accelerations in social mobility, the unquestionable atomisation of social life – even more so in the Covid19 Pandemic – and perhaps the artificiality and self-obsession introduced by the more recent wave of hand-held devices. The onward march of technology can be seen to enable many to live and get fulfilment in predominantly 'virtual' terms.[1]

Taylor considers that these trends bring nothing new: he thinks that such conflicts have always existed; it is just that it now seems easier for the ties with others to be discarded. The issue is how to challenge and combat the situation. Taylor's earlier discussion of the changed view on 'horizons of significance' gives the roadmap of a solution, both as a diagnostic and as the revision towards which Taylor is working.

However, Taylor does not reapply that analysis; instead, he refers to 'social change', which he says has been on a wider scale than formally – and presumably at a faster pace. This has contributed to the deviations in the ethic of authenticity, and if that is to be reversed, the nature of the changes in society must be taken into account.

The focus of much in modernity is on a 'single-minded pursuit of self-development' without the usual regard to the 'obligations' to family or 'allegiance' to wider causes or interests. This raises an obvious question: how and why has this come about?

---

[1] As in many 'live' events, where individuals are more concerned to record the event on a mobile device than to participate in it.
Presumably, they record others recording others recording others, *ad infinitum*.

Historical Backgrounds – Social Mobility and Related Problems

To explore this further, Taylor sketches a political and economic history, somewhat reminiscent of his earlier history of the 'Sources of Authenticity' (Section III). He suggests that from the seventeenth century, we can trace the rise of individualism in developing societies and in European thought, there is the rise of the worldwide market based on individual entrepreneurship.[1] These trends root individualism into everyday life and link it into the emerging package of aspirational values, and this gives rise to the move to deviate from the ideal of the ethic of authenticity: this emerges as the individual's self-fulfilment starts to make instrumental means to personal ends. Taylor notes that there is greater 'social *atomism*' (p. 58), wherein self-development is seen as fulfilment 'just of the self', and a self-orientated flow of anthropocentrism whereby all 'affiliations' of history, tradition, nature, society are seen as dispensable means to the optimal end of the individual's fulfilment.

Taylor takes a particular look at the phenomenon of social mobility, which he says 'is in a sense forced on us' (p. 59). He has in mind that traditional commitments are diminished or lost as people increasingly move to reside and work in larger cities and take on jobs that might mean further moves, leading to greater dislocations. He thinks this leads to the impersonal and atomised setting for life that is such a feature of modernity in developed and developing societies. Instrumental thinking becomes more or less the norm. All of this is enhanced by the technical and bureaucratic elements of society. It is the atomised individual who is thus manifest with a subjective orientation, and this gives rise to the pressure always to have a 'quick fix' (p. 60), to have the

---

[1] The classic example would be the social and economic changes brought through the industrial revolution in Britain, although Taylor does not mention this.

gratification of wants paraded as real needs, and so on.

Furthermore, for Taylor, none of this is true to the ideal of authenticity. Nor is a deviation from that ideal wholly explained by social factors. Taylor also thinks that there are problems that are 'internal to the ideal of self-fulfilment'.

Once more, Taylor packages these as two problems, and again he thinks them to be interrelated with 'complex, criss-crossing relations.'

First, there is the inclination of self-fulfilment to lead individuals to become self-centred – a factor noted earlier but now seen as a problem inherent in the ideal. With the second point, Taylor moves into a new line of thought, suggesting that 'high' culture has been made nihilistic in character due to the removal of 'horizons of significance.' He again takes up the issue of Nietzsche's influence to explore this point.

Nietzsche's critique of values and the nihilistic option links with his incomplete project to 'revalue all values'. As an enterprise, Taylor sees this as critical importance because it promotes the creative will of the individual as the imperative force in and for life.[1] The imperatives of revaluation suggest that the individual is free to will creatively against a backdrop of no values, no horizon of meaning – as in the 'death of God' passage quoted earlier. Taylor refers to Nietzsche and other more recent 'post-modern' thinkers, Derrida and Foucault.[2] These writers present variations on the themes of modernity to portray a creative and highly personalised mode of self-authentication with 'a certain patina of deeper philosophical

---

[1] Again, I have written elsewhere on Nietzsche's project of reversing or revaluing all values – see Loxton (2021), especially Chapter 16.
[2] Taylor refers to J. Derrida (1930-2004) and M. Foucault (1926-1984). As can be seen from the text, Derrida was still alive and active when Taylor wrote: Foucault had died seven years earlier.

justification' (p. 61).

Here Taylor is treading lightly around a tradition of thought he is much more emphatically critical of in *Sources*. The problem is, he suggests there, grounded in a one-sided reading of Nietzsche as made by the modern French school of thought, whereby 'the arbitrariness of interpretation' has been emphasised at the expense of Nietzsche's affirmative teaching.[1] This interpretation leads to a definite promotion of 'the potential freedom and power of the self' as well as a move towards 'a world of equals in mutual recognition'. Taylor thinks that this project of deconstruction gives nothing but a 'flux', a 'kind of unrestrained, utterly self-related freedom'.[2]

Against this one-sided deviation, in *Authenticity*, Taylor wants to say that the nihilistic deviant forms of the ideal of authenticity, and the true and appropriate dialogic form, are all from the same original ideal. Rhetorically he asks, 'How could this be?' (p. 61).

What Taylor wants to do is to make explicit what has surely been clear since he first advanced the idea that these were deviant forms of the ideal – for it is difficult to deviate, save from a prior view, state, or condition.

Accordingly, Taylor argues again that the deviant form of the ideal of ethical authenticity is a distorted form of the true ideal, which means that the true and deviant forms have much in common. However, to argue for the true as against the deviant versions, the idea is that the true form needs to be reformulated, presumably in a manner that offers a better safeguard against future risks of deviation.

---

[1] *Sources* p. 488. I certainly think that Nietzsche's affirmative teaching is some way away from the line given by the French deconstructionists. Again I have written on Nietzsche's ideas separately – Loxton (2021).
[2] *Sources* p. 489.

148

Taylor moves to elucidate what is better through references to artistic creativity.

Analogies with Artistic Creativity

Taylor sets off on this task with a comparison between self-discovery and artistic creation. Following Herder's idea that we each have an original and distinctive way to discover what it is to be human, he says that this 'entails that each of us has to discover what it is to be ourselves' (p. 61). Self-discovery cannot be done 'by consulting pre-existing models, by hypothesis. So it can be made only by articulating it afresh'. We have to become participants in this expressive process:

'We discover what we have it in us to be by becoming that mode of life, by giving expression in our speech and action to what is original in us'.

Taylor suggests that in this process, there is 'a close analogy, even a connection, between self-discovery and artistic creation'. Keeping Herder in mind, Taylor evokes 'the expressivist understanding of human life' (p. 61-62), through which the insight into the relationship between being human and being expressive or creative 'becomes very intimate' (p. 62). He notes how in various aspects of the Romantic movement through the seventeenth and eighteenth centuries, this relation led to artistic creativity becoming 'the paradigm mode in which people come to self-definition' with the artist 'becoming in some way the paradigm case of the human being, as agent of original self-definition'. Taylor links this development to a shift in the wider theory of art, whereby the emergent expressivism rejects the traditional notion of art as a form of imitation (*mimēsis*), favouring the artist as a creator and so as one who represents 'the essence of the human condition' and who operates as 'the creator of cultural values'. As in art, so in life:

'If we become ourselves by expressing what we're about, and if what we become is by hypothesis original, not based on the pre-existing, then what we express is not an imitation of the pre-existing either, but a new creation. We think of the imagination as creative.'

To press this point, Taylor lays on another term from the inescapable cultural horizon of classical Greece, explaining that the new artistic process of self-discovery involves creativity – '*poiēsis*' – in the sense of working to bring out of oneself something new. The core idea is that if we act creatively through the making of something new, we go through a process of self-discovery and so self-development.

Here the difference is as between what happens if, on the one hand, someone assembles a piece of self-build furniture, a functional job, however satisfying, and, on the other, a person working to create something new, embodying themself in the process of creative writing, composing through music or painting. By creating and making anew, a person engages in 'artistic creativity', which, as Taylor says, 'becomes the paradigm mode' for individual 'self-definition'.

Taylor has a clear conviction that because self-discovery and thus authenticity are creative, there is a fusion of the artistic and the moral dimensions, as in the various ways in which the ethic of authenticity is seen to be grounded in a rejection of mere obedience to external orders or standards reflecting society, history and tradition. Taylor notes that 'authenticity will have to struggle' (p. 63) in resisting '*some* externally imposed rules' to achieve 'harmony with the *right* rules'.

Taylor expresses much of this in the following passage:

'… I discover myself through my work as an artist, through what I create. My self-discovery passes through a creation, the making of something original and new. I forge a new artistic language – a new way of painting, new metre or form of poetry, new way of writing a novel – and through this and through this alone I become what I have it in me to be' (p. 62).

This line of thought confirms that authenticity embraces a form of autonomy – living in control of oneself – not living in a condition of heteronomy – living under the control of others. However, in the real tension is to discern that there 'two kinds of demand' (p. 63) that have to be distinguished, both being of importance to the project of retrieving the ideal: there are 'the demands of self-truth and the demands of right treatment that we… accord to others': both 'truth to self' and the demand of 'intersubjective justice' matter.

Taylor elects to explore this issue here by seeing how 'the demands of authenticity are linked in with 'the aesthetic' – by which he means that in philosophical aesthetics, there is work to show how the power of creative art is truly found, not through portrayal as in more traditional art, but through the feelings and responses evoked by the work in question.[1] These ideas developed in the Romantic movement most emphatically in Kant's aesthetic theory in his *Critique of Judgment* (1790).

The ideas that Taylor puts attention on concern how certain feelings and responses come into play as the work is developed through the commitment and development of the artist. It is this that leads to the idea that the meaning and worth of a piece of art is distinctive through its capacity to arouse feelings of aesthetic worth in the person experiencing the art:

---

[1] In the text, Taylor alludes to Shaftsbury and Hutcheson: he means Anthony Ashley Cooper, 3rd Earl of Shaftesbury (1671-1713) and Francis Hutcheson, (1694-1746). Both wrote on the relation between aesthetics and the moral sense. Key works here would be Shaftesbury's *Characteristiks of Men, Manner and Opinions* (1711) and Hutcheson's *An Inquiry into the Original of our Ideas of Beauty and Virtue* (1725).

'Beauty gives its own intrinsic fulfilment. Its goal is internal' (p. 64).

The ethical ideal of authenticity can be seen to work in much the same way, with the internalisation of the sense of value. There is a 'shift in the centre of gravity of the moral demand on us: self-truth and self-wholeness are seen more and more not as means to be moral, independently defined, but as something valuable for their own sake'. (p. 64-65)

Taylor illustrates this by reference to the German writer Schiller's *Letters on the Aesthetic Education of Man*.[1] What Taylor likes in Schiller is how 'the enjoyment of beauty give us a unity and wholeness beyond the divisions that arise in us from the struggle between morality and desire' (p. 65).

With Schiller's ideas in mind, Taylor notes that while there is an affinity between the ethic of authenticity and aesthetic appreciation, there is also the difference that aesthetic wholeness 'engages us totally in a way that morality cannot'. Aesthetic wholeness 'is an independent goal, with its own *telos*, its own form of goodness and satisfaction'. The implication is that if we lose sight of the differences here, we have the agenda and rationale to explain how the deviant form of authenticity can develop: the deviant form immerses itself in creative individuality and embraces the aesthetic of self-creation to the exclusion of the wider horizons and the dialogic relations with others.

The analogies with artistic creativity and self-development also inform the tension that Taylor is alert to between traditional morality and 'the demands of authenticity' as an ethical ideal. Morality, in many traditional instances, is

---

[1] J.C.F von Schiller (1759-1805), writer, thinker, critic and dramatist, Schiller is well-known for the 'Ode to Joy' that Beethoven used as the text for the last movement of his 9th Symphony, the 'Choral Symphony. Taylor refers to Schiller (1967). Taylor writes more on these matters in *Sources* pp. 421-423.

manifest as being 'inseparable from stifling convention' against which the originality and creativity of authenticity comes as 'a revolt'. The usual approach of moralities is to remove from the individual 'much that is elemental and instinctive in us, many of our deepest and most powerful desires'. Taylor sees that this explains why there is, within modernity, a moral reaction against morality, as in the critiques of Nietzsche and others. Taylor does not think that a plurality of authenticities is within the remit of the restoration on which he is working. Too many of the post-modern innovators of forms of authenticity are antagonistic to 'horizons of significance' (p. 66), and so promoting one-sided deviant forms of the ideal.

Taylor then offers (p. 67) a recapitulation:

Authenticity (A) involves (i)'creation', 'construction' and 'discovery'; it entails (ii) 'originality' and often (iii) 'opposition' to rules and conventions.
Authenticity (B) also requires (i)'openness to horizons of significance', so creativity has a background and setting, and it involves (ii) dialogical 'self-definition'.

Here 'A' and 'B' entail a tension – but if 'A' is exalted over 'B' the 'understanding of value as created gives a sense of freedom and power', and Taylor thinks that all the evidence of the twentieth century shows too great and dangerous a 'fascination with violence' due to 'a love affair with power'. Taylor knows that there is a tension between the creative and the more referential aspects of authenticity, in the sense that self-definition emerges from a form of conflict with existing conventions and 'social conformity' (p. 63), then we have the sense that 'authenticity will have to struggle against *some* externally imposed rules'. The trick is, as we noted earlier, to see that the ideal of authenticity entails 'two kinds of demand', which have 'a notional difference', meaning they are different aspects of what is involved in the ideal. There is the demand of 'truth to self' where creativity

153

will be a prominent feature, and the demand of 'intersubjective justice' – which here is Taylor's instance of an 'inescapable horizon' for responsible dialogic life.

From this, we see that in the development of the ideal of authenticity, both aspects of the ideal need to be sustained; both the creative as well as the referential planes have to be held together. If either extreme predominates, the result is a deviant form of authenticity. Taylor again notes a sense of the strains of deviation in modern theories of 'deconstruction' (p. 67). He dwells on this, seeing in this movement an appreciation of the importance of the articulation of language and of aspects of life that go beyond the technical and scientific. However, in this postmodernity, creativity and individualism is exalted to the exclusion of the referential plane – horizons are obliterated, and as far as Taylor is concerned, this can only lead to deviant forms of authenticity. The 'neo-Nietzschean theories' certainly promote 'a sense of radical freedom', and Taylor sees this as a reminder of the importance within authenticity of a measure of 'self-determining freedom':

'Authenticity is itself an idea of freedom; it involves my finding the design of my life myself, against the demands of external conformity' (p. 67-68).

Taylor sees this as giving 'the basis... for an alliance', as between creative individuality and horizons of significance. The problem is that in many cases, the drive of self-determinism has resulted in 'extreme forms of anthropocentrism' (p. 68), not just the individualism of the deconstructionists but also as in the outcomes of the theory and practice of Rousseau, Marx and Lenin. The regimes associated with the latter operators have, Taylor thinks, given rise to far more damaging 'human-centredness' and 'ecological aggressiveness' than 'capitalist' societies.

Taylor concludes this part of his reflection with the health warning that authenticity cannot 'go all the way with self-

154

determining freedom' as to do so would lead to too extreme an anthropocentric view, 'abolishing all horizons of significance' and so 'threatening a loss of meaning' and so a 'trivializing of our predicament'. The Bloomian image of flattening is redeployed: the originality and creativity of authenticity, the drive for being true to oneself, can lead to the insight that 'our situation' as one of 'high tragedy, alone in a silent universe, without intrinsic meaning, condemned to create value'. But then, the flattening realisation is that reality having no value means that there are 'no very meaningful choices' and no really 'crucial issues'.

Taylor ends with a clear warning that appropriately orientated self-determining freedom is a vital aspect of authenticity, but it can also become its 'bane' (p. 69) due to the risk of an over-elaboration of the power of individual choice. If the only value we notice 'is choice itself', we subvert 'both the ideal of authenticity and the associated ethic of recognizing difference'. This latter ethic is connected with the here understated but implied horizons of significance.

Reading/Revision Questions Section VI – *The Slide to Subjectivism*

Makes notes to define, illustrate and explain the following:

1. Taylor adds to the idea of narcissism at the start of this Section: what is the emergent view, and to what contrast does this lead?

2. Taylor reviews how it is that authenticity can 'deviate into the trivial'. What does he suggest to explain this?

3. How does instrumental rationality fortify 'social *atomism*'?

4. Does the modern industrial, technocratic and bureaucratic society help or hinder the ideal of authenticity?

5. Outline and compare the two slides to subjectivism to which Taylor refers.

6. What is the relationship between 'authenticity' and 'originality'?

7. What is the importance to Taylor of the contrast between *mimēsis* and *poiēsis*?

8. What ideas does Taylor take about authenticity from writers on aesthetics, especially Schiller?

9. To what extent does Taylor think authenticity can develop in a diverse manner?

10. Taylor suggests component dimensions of authenticity, set out as (A) and (B). Why must one not privilege (A) over (B) or vice versa?

8. On 'La Lotta Continua' – Section VII

The Section's Title

In this section, Taylor is interested in the question of whether, for the lives of people in the here and now, ideals can be actual and as significant as he wants for the recharged ideal of authenticity. He uses as his title a slogan – *La Lotta Continua* – meaning 'the struggle goes on', which was associated with the Italian extremist Red Brigades of the 1970s. Taylor refers to them as a 'revolutionary' movement (p. 78), but they would probably be best classified as a terrorist organisation. In the text, they are presented as a left-wing Marxist/Leninist revolutionary movement. However they may be described, they operated clandestinely, going to war against Italian society with various acts of sabotage, kidnapping, and murder. The group's most infamous act was the kidnap and murder of a former Italian Prime Minister, Aldo Moro, in 1978.[1] By the late 1980s, the Italian police had arrested and successfully prosecuted the members of the Red Brigades. Given Taylor's regard for the harmonic notion of dialogic relations, the Red Brigades are an unusual source for him to draw on.

A Work of Retrieval and Persuasion

In this section, we carry on with the issues held together at the end of 'The Slide to Subjectivism'. There is some tension in the opening theme, as we are reminded that the wider 'culture of authenticity' entails 'narcissistic' variants on the ideal, and 'properly understood' the ideal condemns the deviant forms. Taylor wants to defend the creative tension between the true ideal and the generalised deviant form that tends towards egotistical indulgence. As we

---

[1] Aldo Moro (1916-1978). Moro twice served as Italian premier – 1963-68 and 1974-76.

know, he thinks that the ideal has a viable true form, hence his desire to defend it.

The truth of the ideal of authenticity comes through its relationship with 'one of the important potentialities of human life', namely the capacity for a 'more self-responsible form of life' (p. 74). This is a theme that has underpinned much of Taylor's thinking in *Authenticity*, and he wants to use it now to aid in retrieving the ideal from the devalued sense of it some critics have, who fuse it with the indulgence of misplaced self-fulfilment. To this end, Taylor argues that a proper grasp of authenticity shows that self-fulfilment includes, indeed it requires, 'unconditional relationships' and 'moral demands beyond the self' (p. 72-73). These points give generalised instances of shape and form to the ethics of authenticity, and they clearly play well on the 'general feature of human life' that Taylor brought into focus earlier, the 'fundamentally dialogic character' (pp. 32-33) of the human condition.

The emphasis that Taylor's book has now becomes explicit: it is not over a simple issue of whether one is for or against authenticity. Taylor is clear that both poles in the debate over authenticity are mistaken. As in Hegelian thought, we are confronted by the extremes of thesis and antithesis. Both the 'knockers' and the 'boosters', as Taylor continues to call the critics and enthusiasts, 'are wrong' (p. 72). In this, the key task is that of 'fighting over the meaning of authenticity' and working to 'persuade people that self-fulfilment, so far from excluding unconditional relationships and moral demands beyond the self, actually requires these in some form' (p. 72-73). This means that there should not be debate '*over* authenticity' – in terms of the pros and cons as expressed by the 'boosters' and 'knockers'– but rather a struggle '*about* it, defining its proper meaning' (p. 73). As in a Hegelian synthesis, we are to avoid the polarities and see a way of getting clear the right and proper sense of authenticity. This is why Taylor likes to describe the process both as 'a work of retrieval' (p. 72) and as 'a work of persuasion', operating to show how we can properly define and grasp the restored ideal of authenticity.

To support the task of persuasive retrieval, Taylor harks back to the points he made at the end of Section II:

'(1) that authenticity is truly an ideal worth espousing; (2) that you can establish in reason what it involves; and (3) that this kind of argument can make a difference in practice' (p. 73).

This last point is where the idea that the text is a 'work of persuasion' comes into play. In contrast to the worry about the extent of the 'inarticulate debate' discussed earlier, Taylor endorses the hope that those he wants to engage with are not 'so locked in by the various social developments that condition them to, say, atomism and instrumental reason that they couldn't change their minds no matter how persuasive you were'.

Taylor thinks the previous section has dealt with issue (2) and shown that the ideal of authenticity can be rationally defined. He proposes to examine issue (3) in the next section, so he now proposes to consider the first issue, that authenticity can be advanced as a worthy ideal.

The Worth of Authenticity

Taylor concedes that he has written much more on the patterns of development of the modern sense of self-identity in *Sources*. He then moves on to explain briefly that the true ideal of authenticity has the value and worth of creating a greater sense of self-responsibility: 'It allows us to live (potentially) a fuller and more differentiated life' (p. 74).

The ideal of authenticity enables a life that is 'more fully appropriated to as our own.' It enables a 'richer mode of existence' as we are challenged to 'work out our own opinions and beliefs for ourselves'. These are positive

161

affirmations to enrich our sense of the content of the ethics of authenticity, although the statements are all somewhat generalised. An assumption in Taylor's exposition is that authenticity as an ideal flows into modernity through the two-hundred-year period since the Enlightenment. This is a cultural and historical period that has greatly encouraged and rewarded the rise of individualism. Taylor thinks that 'everybody in our culture feels the force of this idea', not least, those who are critical of it – the 'knockers', as they are still termed. As the critics see the ideal of authenticity, albeit in its debased form, it presents as 'nonsense' or 'self-indulgence'. Taylor thinks that many who see the ideal as nonsense do so from the perspective of 'a hard-line scientistic attitude to the world'. From this outlook, the language of 'self-fulfilment or authenticity can seem… vague and woolly'. Bloom, as a slight contrast, is representative of humanistic critics. As we have seen, he characterises the modern trends of the ideal as a form of 'moral laxity' (p.75) and a 'loss of the more stringent ideals formally dominant in our culture'.

Despite the force of these criticisms, Taylor retains positivity about the value of the ideal and the worth of the mission of persuasion. He thinks that in modernity, the definition of 'the cultural mainstream of Western liberal society' is made 'in terms of those who feel the draw' of the 'main forms of individualism'. The argument is that even those who are committed to science, or humanism, still operate in their decision-making over careers or life choices with references to parts of the ideal, for their choices are invariably made with reference to fulfilling potential or achieving personal development, or self -realisation.

Taking these trends and values into account, they are not, as such, an argument for the '*worth* of the ideal', but Taylor suggests that it should 'induce some humility' into those who oppose the ideal. He also thinks another question arises: should we not consider 'in *our* situation', the strategy of 'espousing the ideal at its best and trying to raise our practice up to this level'. Here, the reference to 'our practice', our way of living, relating, acting and doing, is again akin to the ethos and style of the virtue thought that Taylor never wants to endorse.

Recalibrating the Task of Persuasion

In the final pages of the section, Taylor offers a rejig of the situation and the task ahead. The modern situation sees a rise of 'the more self-centred forms of fulfilment' (p. 76). People live in relationships that are more readily seen as 'revocable'. Divorce rates seem to be rising, but the other issue is the increasing number of unmarried people who live together. People are less rooted, more mobile, and within democratic societies, there is the worrying 'fall-off in citizen participation'. These factors cause 'alarm', and Taylor rehearses a number of the concerns that come to expression through the life that is a feature of the trend towards 'sheer egoism': the increase in 'mobility', and that more and more of the jobs we do are either instrumental in character or involve our manipulation of others. But if these 'self-centred' forms of life are seen through the lens of authenticity, 'an ineradicable tension' can be felt, coming from 'the sense of an ideal that is not being fully met in reality. This gives scope for the continuation of the struggle to 'articulate the shortfall of practice and criticize it' (p. 77).

What Taylor thinks is that if we consider even the self-related trends going on in the emergent liberal and pluralist culture of modernity, where all kinds of options and all kinds of frameworks of meaning might be used to reference the various life projects in evidence, nevertheless, within these, the thread of the ideal of authenticity is found. This suggests to Taylor that even the critics should consider why that is. Against this suggestion, the critic might argue that the richness, diversity and the related benefits of a liberal pluralist culture, one that is positive in its soft relativism, are the consequence of the true development of the ethics of authenticity. In other words, Taylor distorts this himself when he aims to locate the ethics of authenticity through allegiance to various horizons of significance. Taylor considers that in 'recent decades' – given his previous references to Bloom, he means in all probability the 1960s, 70s and 80s – the self-centred deviant mode of the ideal of authenticity has been prevalent – yet the deviant mode of life presupposes the original from which that deviation is made – and this gives Taylor his restorative hope.

If we imagine abandoning the true ideal, the self-centred trend could well become inexorable. However, if, as Taylor wants, we see the trend as a variant of the true ideal, we can see the general condition as one where there are tensions, as discussed in the previous section. Thus modernity gives a partial exhibition of the true ideal. This provides a setting with a rationale to contest the case for a stronger move towards a fuller expression of both the ideal and the ethics of authenticity. Taylor comes to his suggestion – we have referenced it before – that the true ideal of authenticity 'opens an age of responsibilization', by which he means a situation where people become self-fulfilling in aspiration and aware of being more and more responsible for that process. There are risks, such as the heights of selfishness or the depths of self-indulgence. Taylor is firm on assailing highly ideological total solutions, such as may be associated with Marxism and continues to affirm that the struggle is worthwhile and must go on, which brings us back to why he likes the section's title, *La Lotta Continua.* Taylor says he is neither pessimistic (thinking that there is no hope for cultural progress) nor optimistic (thinking things will always get better); he thinks there is a struggle ahead but one where there is a good case to promote the positive and true ideal of authenticity.

Taylor draws attention to the features of modern society that can, he thinks, be especially problematic – he mentions 'alienation and bureaucratic rigidity' (p. 78). These trends can fuel pessimism about modernity, just as an over-idealised environmentalist line of thought can be over-optimistic. Taylor makes the contrasts here to restate his persuasive campaign that looks to 'break with our temptation to discern irreversible trends, and see that there is a struggle here, whose outcome is continually up for grabs' (p. 79). Taylor puts in further thought to expose what he considers to be the 'counter-productive' influence of the pessimistic critics of authenticity. He has in mind those with 'a disengaged scientistic outlook' as well as 'those with more traditional ethical views, as well as some proponents of an outraged high culture'. Here is an 'alliance of people' who 'unite to condemn this culture'. Taylor rejects this alliance as having an altogether too negative approach. As a counter, he urges a more participatory approach, to 'enter sympathetically into the animating ideal and to try to show what it really requires'. The stand-off between the critics and supporters of the ideal of authenticity gets so bound up with the debate for and against that they lose sight of 'a rich understanding of this ideal' (p. 80), and it against this that Taylor's struggle of persuasion and 'retrieval' has to be conducted.

***Reading/Revision Questions* Section VII** – *La Lotta Continua.*

Makes notes to define, illustrate and explain the following:

1. What does 'La Lotta Continua' mean? Why does Taylor like this as a theme?

2. What views of the culture of authenticity are set out at the start of the Section?

3. What can we infer about Taylor's outlook from his view that his book is 'a work of persuasion'?

4. Why does Taylor think that the struggle between modernity's 'boosters and knockers' is itself a mistake? What should both sides be fighting over? How is that different?

5. What does Taylor add to our sense of 'the worth of the ideal' of authenticity?

6. Do you agree with Taylor that the ideal of authenticity 'points us towards a more self-responsible form of life'?

7. How persuasive is Taylor's suggestion that authenticity opens an 'age of responsibilization'?

8. Why does Taylor think it appropriate for a 'genuinely free society' to take on the slogan 'la lotta continua'?

9. In the campaign to restore the ethical ideal of authenticity, why does Taylor propose an ongoing struggle, not a quick dash for victory?

9. On 'Subtler Languages' – Section VIII[1]

'Subjectivation', *'Manner'* and *'Matter'* in Modernity

At the start of this section, Taylor's final section dealing with the first malaise of individualism, another diagnostic term is brought to bear: 'subjectivation' (p. 81). Taylor deploys this to characterise 'a many-faceted movement' running through various strands of modernity whereby all kinds of things previously referenced to some 'external reality' – the 'horizons of significance', no doubt – are now matters for appropriation, assessment and deployment within and by the individual subject: the idea is that 'we have to think it out for ourselves':

'Modern freedom and autonomy centres us on ourselves, and the ideal of authenticity requires that we discover and articulate our own identity'.

Up to a point, as a trend in modernity, 'subjectivation' is important since it has the effect of basing freedom and autonomy on the individual subject requiring that we 'discover and articulate our own identity'. A central aspect of the ideal of authenticity is here represented, and we might think that Taylor considers this a very good thing. However, with the theme of *La Lotta Continua* ringing in our ears, we can perhaps guess that Taylor sees an ongoing struggle and will not be fully endorsing the growing trend towards 'subjectivation'. He does, however, add an important distinction.

The suggestion is that one facet of modernity's trend over how people find and express their identity has to do with what we choose and what then we actually do, so this leads to the distinction between the '*manner*' and the '*matter* or *content* of action' (p. 82). The 'manner' – 'matter'

---

[1] 'Subtler Languages' is the title for the fifth part of *Sources*: pp. 393-493.

distinction, as the second clause's rider suggests, is akin to a 'form' versus 'content' distinction, where *how* people discover and achieve their identity is one thing, but *what* they choose is another. This distinction is something we need to illustrate.

Suppose that a person living in the UK needs a new car to commute from their rural home to a nearby town: there are no trains or buses, so a car is needed. They have the means to buy a new car and could choose a powerful sporty vehicle that would also be fun to drive. Alternatively, they could buy a larger SUV with lots of practical benefits. However, both of these vehicles will use either petrol or diesel fuel and will all-round, emit more undesirable pollutants than is ideal. Here, the person driven by the 'manner' of self-affirmation alone might still purchase one or other of these vehicles. Someone also motivated by the 'matter' of choice would, on Taylor's thinking, look at the larger picture – the political, economic, environmental and ethical picture (or 'horizons') – and then think that a hybrid or an electric vehicle might well serve better.

We must be clear that Taylor's view is that the operating ethos of the ideal of authenticity needs this dimension of the '*manner*' of self-referential autonomy. Authentic choosing must be in the form or style of being 'self-referential' (p. 82) to represent the orientation of the chooser, the subject. The idea here is, as in our example, that the individual must take the plunge and accept that in the business of volition, of making choices, the responsibility is theirs: so they must decide which car must be bought. However, this does not mean that the content or '*matter*' of the choice has to be self-referential: a self-referential choice can be orientated to 'God, or a political cause, or tending the earth'. Variously inescapable horizons are entailed here, and this, the relational, or as Taylor has it, dialogic orientation is where the subject will find 'genuine fulfilment' – and as in our example, a viable new car.

Taylor's view is that in modernity, too many people have glossed over the difference between these two modes of self-referentiality. The great error, as he sees it from his earlier discussions – is to assume from the *manner* of self-referential autonomy that the *matter* chosen is validated by the *manner* of the choice. The 'catastrophic' outcome is the 'worst forms of subjectivism'. The damaging approach is when people say that all is well with what they have done because they made their own decision. Unless what they have chosen through this process is factored in, problems arise along the perilous lines of self-indulgence, narcissism, and the slide into subjectivity, such as Taylor has portrayed them.

Again – and as in Sections IV and VI – Taylor opts to illustrate the point with the example of art. In this case, he considers writers in the 'development of modern art' to draw out the crucial difference between the two forms of self-referential choice. He clarifies that the operational rule for the ethics of authenticity is that the *manner* of self-referential choice is a given, but so is the issue of the *matter* of what is chosen.

Taylor's idea is that whether in literature or the fine arts, past artistic endeavours operated creatively but also referentially within accepted commonly held systems of value. This meant that such works had and could allude to publicly acknowledged points of reference. However, in the characteristic modes of modernity, the emphasis has changed, and artistic activity is much more seen as the expression of a personal vision or response. There may or may not be a referential connection, or the work may be programmatic. We cannot now assume that it is referential to that which is commonly shared with the tradition of artistic work, not least because, in the plural modernity, commonality is elusive and akin to a Chimera. The likes, tastes and passions of individuals are highly variable; it is an altogether more complex business to work in this non-referential and more expressive mode of creativity. As the title of the section suggests, 'subtler languages' will be needed and will need to be interpreted.

Illustrations from Pope and Shelley

Taylor makes another foray into styles of creativity, such as he considered in Section VI. He refers to a series of writers to illustrate his point, considering Shakespeare, Baudelaire and Rilke, to show how in literature there was a move from a certain reliance on '*mimēsis*' (p. 82), how artistic representation draws on, copies and represents reality, to a mode of activity and work 'that stresses creation' – we are back with the notion of *poiēsis* again. Great artists manage this fusion of manner and matter and can develop creative and empowering interpretations. The message Taylor takes from this is that, in the long run, the rest of us need to embrace this fusion.

The points that he wants to develop emerge clearly in the contrasts made between the poetic work of Alexander Pope and Percy Bysshe Shelley.[1]

Taylor's point is that Pope, working in the seventeenth and eighteenth centuries, 'could draw on age-old views of the order of nature as a commonly available source of poetic images' (p. 84), as in his poem *Windsor Forest*. In contrast, Shelley, working in the later Romantic period, has the motivation to 'articulate his own world of references, and make them believable'.

To see what Taylor means, we can look at *Windsor Forest* and also reference the review made in *Sources*, where Pope's *Essay on Man* is examined. We can also look at one of Shelley's poems.

---

[1] Alexander Pope (1688-1744); Percy Bysshe Shelley (1782-1822).

When Taylor considers Pope's *Essay on Man*, he cites some passages which emphasise the ease with which Pope can write with referential sense to a 'vision of order', to a 'great chain of being'.[1]

Thus:

> 'Vast chain of being! From which God began,
> Natures ethereal, human, angel, man
> Beast, bird, fish, insect, what no eye can see,
> No glass can reach; from infinite to thee,
> from thee to Nothing.'

Then:

> 'All are but parts of one stupendous whole,
> Whose body Nature is, and God the soul'.

The point that Taylor sees in this is encapsulated in another line: 'All Nature is but Art, unknown to thee'.[2]

What Taylor draws out of this is that Pope is writing in and for a tradition he participated in, where there is a sense of order, which Taylor explains:

'The order we are being asked to admire here is not an order of expressed or embodied meanings. What makes the collection of entities that make up the world into an order is not primarily that they realise an interrelated whole of possibilities... The principle thing that makes the entities in the world into an order is that their natures *mesh*'.[3]

Taylor's notion of meshing here is central to the idea he has that our lives need the dialogic style of relationship, as well

---

[1] *Sources* p. 274. Taylor quotes from Pope's *Essay on Man*, I. 237-241 and 267-268.

[2] *Sources* p. 275, quoting Pope's *Essay* I. 289.

[3] *Sources* p. 275.

as an orientation to inescapable horizons. Pope's *Windsor Forest* gives further examples of the valued harmony and interlocking coherence that Taylor appreciates.

Windsor Forest is a long poem, so we will quote just a few lines to illustrate how Pope unfolds his muse: Pope, who was born in London but who knew Windsor and its forest well, wrote the poem over several years, and it was first published in 1713.

> 'Thy forests, *Windsor*! and thy green retreats...
> Unlock your springs, and open all your shades...
> The groves of *Eden*, vanish'd now so long,
> Live in description, and look green in song:
> These, were my breast inspir'd with equal flame,
> Like them in beauty, should be like in fame.
> Here hills and vales, the woodland and the plain,
> Here earth and water, seem to strive again;
> Not *Chaos* like together crush'd and bruis'd,
> But as the world, harmoniously confus'd:
> Where order in variety we see,
> And where, tho' all things differ, all agree.
> Here waving groves a checquer'd scene display,
> And part admit, and part exclude the day;
> As some coy nymph her lover's warm address
> Nor quite indulges, nor can quite repress.'[1]

In these lines we can note allusions to the book of Genesis, with the references to the Garden of Eden and the chaos out of which came creation.[2] With his reference to nymphs, we have allusions to classicism, and there are more of both types of reference as the poem unfolds. In Taylor's view, what is relevant are the verses that see the world as 'harmoniously confus'd: Where order in variety we see, And where, tho' all things differ, all agree'. Here we have the sense of an order, enmeshed and presented as a coherent process that provides the backdrop (or horizon) for making

---

[1] See Pope (2011) pp. 24-35. The verses quoted are from line 1 – 20.
[2] See Genesis 1-3 – NRSV (2010).

sense of life. Taylor's thought is that when Pope writes this, all these matters of coherence are assumed and held in a common understanding.

Moving to the nineteenth century, the high tide of Romanticism, and Shelley's writings, we find that 'the poet must articulate his own world of references and make them believable' (p. 84). Taylor does not give a specific example from Shelley's works, preferring to cite views on the salient points from Wasserman's study, *The Subtler Language*.[1]

Wasserman explains that in the nineteenth century, the world-view had changed from the time of Pope, so that 'an additional formulative act was required of the poet'.[2] The new scenario means that the modern poet must work to produce work that can 'both formulate its own cosmic syntax and shape the autonomous poetic reality that the cosmic syntax permits', the point being that 'nature' is no longer 'prior to the poem and available for imitation'. Instead, nature 'now shares with the poem a common origin in the poet's creativity'.

Building on this, Taylor notes that the poets of Romanticism – he cites Wordsworth, Hölderlin and then Shelley, all have responses that alert us to 'something in nature for which there are as yet no adequate words' (p. 85).[3]

Taylor's view is that 'the Romantic poets and their successors have to articulate an original vision of the cosmos.' Wordsworth's *The Prelude* is an example of a work where the poet's evocation of nature could no longer

---

[1] See Wasserman (1968).
[2] Wasserman (1968) pp. 10-11 – as quoted by Taylor – *Authenticity* p. 85. Further quotations are from this same source.
[3] William Wordsworth (1770-1850) – eminent British poet – works include *The Prelude* (1805). Friedrich Hölderlin (1770-1843) – German lyric poet.

'play on an established gamut of references'.[1] Instead of the poet logging into established patterns of reference, the inner experiences, intuitions and values of the poet impressed themselves into the process of reading and responding to the experiences of living reality. This new tradition offers novel insights through the shaping of creative means to express sensed and reasoned insights.

The phrase 'subtler languages' as used in the title of Wasserman's book and by Taylor as the title of this section derives from Shelley's poem *The Revolt of Islam*.[2]

The key lines are these:

> 'And on the sand would I make signs to range
> These woofs, as they were woven, of my thought;
> Clear, elemental shapes, whose smallest change
> A subtler language within language wrought:
> The key of truths which once were dimly taught.'

The idea that we can employ a 'subtler language within language' to use as a 'key to truths' to unlock and illuminate new insights is a powerful image of the human capacity for both deeper, self-conscious reflection and for the generation of responses that are creative and innovative. Taylor is wholly approving of this capacity as an elemental aspect of the authentic ideal of authenticity.

To gain insight into what Taylor sees in this new tradition in general, and to Shelley in particular, one poem serves to illustrate. Shelly wrote *Ozymandias* in 1817. He had been reflecting on the news of various discoveries of

---

[1] This is very true of the 1805 text of *The Prelude*, as compared with the far mode subdued version of 1838, first published in 1850. See Wordsworth (1995).
[2] Canto 32 1 3109-3116 online version @ http://www.online-literature.com/shelley_percy/2779/

174

antiquities in Egypt. Amongst these were some relics of Rameses II, one of the Pharaohs of Egypt, who may have been the Pharaoh in the narratives of the book of Exodus. There was also an inscription to 'Ozymandias, King of Kings', and this gave him a wave of inspiration:

Ozymandias[1]

> 'I met a traveller from an antique land,
> Who said—"Two vast and trunkless legs of stone
> Stand in the desert. . . Near them, on the sand,
> Half sunk a shattered visage lies, whose frown,
> And wrinkled lip, and sneer of cold command,
> Tell that its sculptor well those passions read
> Which yet survive, stamped on these lifeless things,
> The hand that mocked them, and the heart that fed;
> And on the pedestal, these words appear:
> My name is Ozymandias, King of Kings;
> Look on my Works, ye Mighty, and despair!
> Nothing beside remains. Round the decay
> Of that colossal Wreck, boundless and bare
> The lone and level sands stretch far away."'

Shelley does not write a poem as a eulogy in broad homage to an ancient culture: his poem uses the device of testimony and the recollection of a meeting to cast the poem in the idiom of an account. As the poem unfolds, what is notable is the impression we get of the artistry of the sculptor evident in the remnants of the statutory, and this is praised for how the character of Ozymandias is revealed. Shelley, a political radical, is no lover of tyrants and so relishes exposing the cold and cruel character of his imagined subject. With the irony that is disclosed as the arrogant inscription – 'Look on my Works, ye Mighty, and despair!' – is held in tension with the desolate waste of the desert – 'Nothing beside remains./ Round the decay/Of that colossal Wreck, boundless and bare/The lone and level sands stretch

---

[1] Online edition @
https://www.poetryfoundation.org/poems/46565/ozymandias

far away' – Shelley also does the very modern thing of exposing the frailty and contingency of human aspirations, and showing in and through his writing, that a more durable insight is evident in the creative, poetic form.

What Taylor wants to draw out with reference to Shelley is that the 'manner' of his innovations linked to the 'matter' of his expressive form is deeply thought and felt, and comes through an enmeshed fusion with wider horizons of meaning: Shelley is not simply operating on an arbitrary whim.

Taylor on Caspar David Friedrich

Taylor moves on to the painter, Caspar David Friedrich, who, like Shelley, is seen as being distinctive through searching for new images to release a personal vision of both life and nature.[1] Taylor says Friedrich sought 'a symbolism in nature not based on the accepted conventions' (p. 86), and that he too was 'seeking a subtler language; he is trying to say something for which no adequate terms exist and whose meaning has to be found in his works rather than in a pre-existing lexicon of references'.

It is easy to endorse this estimate if we consider one of Friedrich's paintings, *The Wanderer above the Sea of Fog* (1818).

Prior to Friedrich painting this, there was a long, vibrant and increasingly lucrative tradition of portraiture. As a rule, the painter portrayed the subject or subjects, as they footed the bill for the painting. Moreover, the subject would be shown front-on, in their most flattering pose and apparel. In Friedrich's work, this aspect of the tradition is cast aside as the subject is reversed and viewed from the rear, and the role of the land and skyscape is enhanced.

---

[1] Caspar David Friedrich (1774-1840).

Casper David Friedrich: *The Wanderer above the Sea of Fog* (1818). As depicted on a German postage stamp in 2011.

We get from the title that the 'Wanderer' has ascended high above the residual level of the mists and clouds of the area and that he is enabled by his singular efforts to see above and beyond the everyday world. Up to a point, we are drawn into a participative sharing of the subject's vision. Perhaps like us, his eye is drawn to the greater peak in the distance – perhaps the challenge for tomorrow. Alone, he looks ahead, and what he sees, aspires to, whether he is optimistic, content, pessimistic, melancholic, we do not, and cannot know. The level of agnosticism in this portrayal is distinctive. The subject is subordinate to the painter's expressive ideal, and it certainly fits the impression Taylor has of modern art operating in novel and expressive ways that also commit to a 'manner' of self-responsible creative and innovating activity, without falling into self-referenced and self-indulgent 'matters' of choice.

This point on the roles of 'manner' and 'matter' and the tie-in with artistic creativity and self-development could be explored through the musical arm of culture over the same period as Taylor takes with many of his artistic examples.

If we were to consider the classical tradition from Haydn, Mozart, Beethoven, and then on through to Schubert, Schumann and Brahms (who embrace the tradition and move it on) and then contrast this with the individualism of Chopin's development of the tradition, or the deliberate development of an alternative tradition of musical art in Liszt and Wagner, we would see ample evidence of creative self-development done referentially to the wider musical, political and cultural horizons.[1]

Taylor does not see these movements in the creative arts as evidence of fragmentation but as a development of personal responses to artistic potentiality. However, he thinks that this development changes the role we have in our appreciation of art.

On the developing view, Taylor suggests, we do not see this style of art as simply representational, so we do not think to check it against the 'reality' it depicts to see how accurate a correspondence is in evidence. Instead, we see this as expressive of the human condition, and as human subjects, we are drawn to engage with the art and re-experience it. Illustrating this, and thinking of writers who are set within modernity, Taylor puts the point as follows: '… what Eliot

---

[1]Within this, there are multiple compositions where authentic creativity is in evidence, yet also in the framework of what we might call musical horizons. For example, how Beethoven produces creative and radical variations on the form of the baroque fugue in his late piano compositions and string quartets is a worthwhile area for further investigation.

or Pound or Proust invites me to has an ineradicably personal dimension' (p. 87).[1]

Wordsworth and the Issue of 'Manner' versus 'Matter'

Going back to the manner – matter distinction drawn at the start of the section, Taylor thinks that he has exemplified subjectivism of manner with the cases he has considered. However, none of the examples entails a necessary slide into subjectivism of matter. On the contrary, each of the writers or artists he has placed in the more modern style of creativity does far more than simply give an 'expression of the self' (p. 88). Each is, as a study of any would quickly show, referencing a range of pertinent historical, literary and philosophical horizons. To illustrate the claims he is developing, Taylor moves to reconsider some of the work of Wordsworth, taking some lines from the poem *Tintern Abbey*:

> 'And I have felt
> A presence that disturbs me with the joy
> Of elevated thoughts; a sense sublime
> Of something far more deeply interfused
> Whose dwelling is the light of setting suns,
> And the round ocean and the living air,
> And the blue sky, and in the mind of man:
> A motion and a spirit that impels
> All thinking things, all objects of all thought,
> And rolls through all things.'[2]

Taylor explains that Wordsworth is often presented as a poet of overflowing feeling, but in a poem like *Tintern*

---

[1] Taylor is referring to the poets T. S. Eliot (1888-1965) and Ezra Pound (1885-1972) and the French writer Marcel Proust (1871-1922), author of *À la recherché du temps perdu* (translated as *Remembrance of Things Past*, or as *In Search of Lost Time*).

[2] Taylor quotes this in *Authenticity* p. 88 – he quotes lines 94-102 of the poem – line 93 is added here, as in Taylor's quotation in *Sources* – p 369 n. 2.

Abbey, the poet is clearly doing much more than simply emote. He is trying to articulate something 'beyond the self'. Taylor, perhaps wisely, does not try to spell out what that is, but it is clear enough from his writings on 'inescapable horizons' that Wordsworth is seen as one in a 'dialogic' relation with a deeper metaphysical perspective.

Taylor touches on some more literary examples and leaves us in no doubt that confusing subjectivity of manner and matter is easy to do; modern art, he says, too often embraces the subjective but so that it only works 'on the celebration of human powers and feelings' (p. 89). We may not now have much metaphysical confidence in the 'Great Chain of Being', but if we see reality as simply 'a source of raw materials for our projects' we will be diminished, as we lose touch with the sense of the deep need of having a relationship with something against which we find out who we are, a 'larger order that can make claims on us.' Taylor suggests that subjectivism in the reductive sense of focusing solely on self-fulfilment lacks the resource to engage in proper dialogue and relationship with this 'larger order'. Then, without the 'languages of personal resonance' (p. 90), there will be serious moral consequences. He is concerned with emphasising that while disengaged reason is a component in the ideal of authenticity, it deviates from the true ideal when it is elaborated as a distinct solution to the human condition.

Taylor's idea is that we need to rise above 'disengaged reason' and pure 'subjectivism' and avoid 'stern' moralism or reactionary approaches; this is done by re-engaging with a part of the romantic movement's enmeshed vision of the way in which 'self-feeling and the feeling of belonging to nature were linked' (p. 91).[1] More than anything, Taylor

---

[1] Here we might recall that Taylor's major works in the earlier part of his career were on the philosopher Hegel (1770-1831), who certainly thought that all of reality operated with this sort of integration.

urges that we cultivate the 'inner sense of that linkage' the better to 'connect to a wider whole' to rightly integrate our 'being true to ourselves'. What this means is that to be true to ourselves, we need to be active and distinct participants in a wider culture of meaning and value. We cannot live long and prosper well if we try to make up life as we go along.

Here Taylor reaches the end of his eighth section, the seventh in which he has explored individualism, the first of the worrying malaises of modernity identified in Section 1. this leaves two sections to cover the other two malaises of instrumental reason and the loss of freedom. In brief, we may say that Taylor has steadily enriched the perspectives within the ethical ideal of authenticity, and his hope is the ideas on the 'manner' and 'matter' of how individualism has been reviewed to the end of reaffirming the ideal of authenticity can be applied to the other two malaises without him having to lead us through all the illustrative detail.

The perspectives drawn on individualism suggest that human life is conditioned by the backdrop of the horizons of significance. Rightly aligned, these empower the moral and creative development of individuality as in the pattern Taylor traces in the earlier sections of his text. We see the continued focus on the intercommunicative role of dialogic relations, which emerge as fundamentally vital to the positive capacity of humans to operate in morally purposeful and creative ways, avoiding the debased options of reacting to the plurality of modernity by retreating to narrow subjectivism or the extremes of absolutism.

Reading/Revision Questions Section VIII *Subtler Languages.*

Makes notes to define, illustrate and explain the following:

1. Illustrate and explain what Taylor means by 'subjectivation'.

2. What is the difference between the 'manner' and the 'matter' of authenticity?

3. Why does Taylor think that confusing these two notions is 'catastrophic'?

4. Why do the 'publicly available reference points' (allusions found in literature or art) no longer hold for us?

5. Explain Shelley's use of the term 'subtler languages'.

6. Track and explain the 'qualitative change in artistic languages' Taylor charts. How is this significant for human self-understanding?

7. What is the 'ineradicably personal dimension' to which authors like T. S. Eliot, Ezra Pound, or Marcel Proust invite Taylor?

8. What is the 'something beyond the self' which modern poets have been attempting to articulate?

9. How does Taylor use the issue of responses to potential ecological disaster to illustrate both the inadequacy of anthropocentrism and the possibility of subtler languages?

10. On 'An Iron Cage?' – Section IX

Instrumental Reason Revisited

In this penultimate section, Taylor re-considers the problem identified as that of instrumental reason. As a reminder, instrumentalism in Taylor's view is any mode of thinking where the end justifies the means, where all is a means to the end of either the greatest number, as in classical forms of utilitarianism, or of the individual in search of egotistical self-fulfilment in cases of distorted variations of the ideal of authenticity. Instrumental reason is also seen to be dominant in economic, technical and scientific enterprises.[1] Given that Taylor thinks he has shown how the distorted variants of the ethics of authenticity can be countered and corrected by the ideal proper, what he now wants to examine is how what has been established in the treatment of individualism can be applied to instrumental reason so that, on a broader front, it can also be challenged.

One issue facing Taylor's project comes from his relish for the notion of philosophical anthropology and for seeing the ethical ideal of authenticity as rooted in a dialogic mode of what it is to be human, with disengaged reason employed to recharge thinking in positive ways. This package is esteemed over and above the means to immediate ends approach of instrumental reason. Nevertheless, we might think that it is through instrumentalist thinking, linked to collaborative, interactive, and indeed, dialogic activity, that humans have brought about technological, economic, medical and scientific innovations having many significant benefits. Despite the snags that Taylor sees in instrumentalism, and his understandable desire to recover certain ends otherwise eclipsed, in attacking instrumental reason, he will have to be careful not to alienate the positives that have enhanced life and authenticity from

---

[1] See for example *Authenticity* pp. 6-7.

instrumentally inclined technical, economic, scientific and medical innovation.

Fortunately, Taylor is alert to the issue, and he recapitulates the view that in respect of instrumental reason, 'there are extreme positions' (p. 94) so that in relation to the ideal of authenticity, it is unwise to go the positions of the enthusiasts and critics he again refers to as 'the boosters and the knockers' (p. 93).

The more valid analysis, and the lesson from the longer consideration of individualism, comes through finding a persuasive balance, in seeing the danger of these extreme forms of self-fulfilment, and the greater value and worth of dialogic self-development. In personal life as well as in cultural terms, Taylor sees the dual dangers of 'systematic cultural pessimism' and 'a global cultural optimism' (p. 94). The ongoing task again involves the sense of the slogan *La Lotta Continua* – it is one of 'a continuing struggle to realize higher and fuller modes of authenticity'. Further modes of self-development and authenticity are possible to overcome the risk of 'flatter and shallower' modes of pure subjectivity.

On instrumental reason, Taylor writes on the various themes of alienation, of how, in modernity, at least as viewed in the early 1990s, a problem is that human life has, through a reliance on technology and instrumentalism in general, lost affinity with and for nature. He means that our broad social disengagement with the fundamental routines of life means that we lose contact with 'ourselves and our own natural being', and instead of this, the enmeshed and embedded dialogic mode of authentic life, we have tended to operate with a dominant perspective over nature. We have come to live and work with knowledge and information about the world, but we have lost our right and properly informed sense of living within and as a part of it. This leads to some reactions where we find a form of nostalgia, as in movements that admire 'pre-industrial peoples', and offer a political defence for 'aboriginal societies against the encroachment of industrial civilisation', and such themes recur, he thinks in feminism's assault on patriarchal trends in society – where patriarchy is seen as the main factor in the human domination of nature. These movements all take issue with those, 'the out-and-out boosters of technology', who think there will always be a technological solution 'for all our human problems' (p. 95).

Taylor makes a number of points about the tensions he sees in modernity. One is that there are what he calls unusual political 'cross-alignments' in the poles of the debate. For example, those who are classified as the 'knockers of authenticity' tend to come from the political right, while those who are knockers of 'technology' are from the left. Some of those who are 'critical of the ethic of self-fulfilment' are highly supportive of 'technological development', while most of those who are 'deeply into the contemporary culture of authenticity share the points made about 'patriarchy and aboriginal styles of life'.

We are led by this to 'some troubling contradictions':

'Right-wing American-style conservatives speak as advocates of traditional communities when they attack abortion on demand and pornography; but in their economic policies they advocate an untamed form of capitalist enterprise, which more than anything else has helped to dissolve historical communities, has fostered atomism, which knows no frontiers or loyalties, and is ready to close down a mining town or savage a forest habitat at the drop of a balance sheet'.

Then, 'on the other side':

'… we find supporters of an attentive, reverential stance to nature, who would go to the wall to defend the forest habitat, demonstrating in favour of abortion on demand, on the grounds that the woman's body belongs exclusively to her'.

The accumulated view is that 'some adversaries of savage capitalism carry progressive individualism farther than its most untroubled defenders'.

More 'Work of Retrieval'

Consistent with his previous discussion of modernity, Taylor avoids taking sides in these debates as he considers the extremes on each side to 'more or less equally wrong' (p. 96). He means each has the balance equally wrong, which means that there are elements on each side that play deeply into how the modern problem of the ideal of authenticity can be understood.

The extreme influence of 'runaway instrumental reason' is found in 'the hardening of an atomistic outlook' and in 'our imperviousness to nature'. The critics of modernity – the 'knockers' – are right to see a problem here. Technological developments within and for a social benefit are possible, but Taylor thinks that 'richer moral sources' will be needed, and these have to be revived from the blurring caused by the atomistic and instrumental trends. As to the 'boosters', they do not help the task of revival because they are so deeply immersed in 'the atomist and instrumental stance'. They assume these and cannot perceive them as 'sources' that might be refined and revised. Accordingly, Taylor thinks that he has to move beyond 'the polarized debate' so as to engage in more of the 'work of retrieval' (p. 97) so that instrumentalism can be seen afresh as a component in the 'fruitful struggle' for the true ideal of authenticity.

Taylor then suggests that before this aspect of the task of retrieval gets underway, there is an unavoidable point to confront. That 'to a considerable degree the dominance of instrumental reason is not just a matter of the force of a certain moral outlook'. It is also that instrumental reason has a significant role in modernity because of the highly advanced technological economy we live in, which prizes efficiency and is driven by pure market forces and the profit motive. This brings many benefits to what we might term the common good. It is also the case that to operate such a system, whether 'we leave our society to "invisible hand" mechanisms like the market or try to manage it collectively' – here Taylor covers the basic range of options in political economy, ranging from the free market to collectivism – we need 'bureaucratic rationality', and this 'modern rationality', which is very instrumental in its operation, becomes something that we cannot dispense with altogether. Instrumental reason in its various forms is nevertheless the force that gives rise to the marginalised atomism of modernity, a much less desirable phenomenon against the criterion of the ideal ethic of authenticity.

It might be argued that instrumental reason is so strongly established as to be an unalterable influence, but Taylor's view is that we can, in fact, combat the dominance of instrumental reason through the attack on the deviant forms of the ethic of authenticity, and that thereby, we can retain a tactical role for the instrumentalism that serves us well, yet escape the reductive 'iron cage' (p. 98) variants of technological reason.

Taylor's reasoning for this adjustment is that 'the view of technological society as a kind of iron fate cannot be sustained'. For one thing, he thinks such a view is too simplistic, and it 'forgets the essential'. The emergent 'philosophies of atomism and instrumentalism' (p. 99) have come partly from the 'institutions'. However, atomism – individualism – and instrumental thinking were in the outlooks 'of western Europe and America before the Industrial Revolution', and Taylor refers to Weber's sense of this 'ideological preparation', which is a slightly oblique and allusive way of saying that atomism and instrumentalism have roots in the Protestant view of individuals being saved by faith alone. To be fair, Taylor does not buy wholly into Weber's account because he makes clear the view that the deeper truth about the traditions that make up modern society is that they, and so modernity itself, are very much more complex than can be explained by any one line of interpretation. He again appeals to 'the Romantic era' and to more recent ecology movements to illustrate this.[1] He thinks that these traditions have also had considerable impact, pervading society, showing how vulnerable we, and indeed nature are, when we are 'fragmented' (p. 100) by instrumentalism, and how what is good and right is to have 'common understanding' and 'common consciousness' to defend and safeguard ourselves and the environment.

An emergent truth lies, Taylor again thinks, in the realisation that human freedom is not absolute. This drives home the critique of subjective individualism, which too easily assumes a form of purer liberality. However, humans are not completely determined either, so we should not fall prey to the mechanistic extremes of instrumentalism. Our grasp of the moral options within our civilization – the refreshed ideal of authenticity being to the fore – can reshape our understanding of progress. Here Taylor redeploys the nuanced notion of self-determining freedom he discussed earlier:

'We are free when we can remake the conditions of our own existence, when we can dominate the things that dominate us' (p. 101).

With a view to his modernity, alluding to the then-recent demise of the Soviet bloc, Taylor comes up with an image of intellectual cladding or veneer, thinking that in western societies, there is better evidence of a capacity to 'enframe

---

[1] Here Taylor might have referred to the influence of the New England Transcendentalists, R. W. Emerson (1803-1882) and H. D. Thoreau (1817-1862). Emerson's *Nature* (1837) and Thoreau's *Walden* (1854) offer ongoing insights antagonistic to the instrumental and atomistic aspects of modernity that Taylor also dislikes.

instrumental reason' so that we dominate it with the higher ethical purpose of the ideal of authenticity, rather than be dominated by a 'runaway technological devastation of the environment'. It may be that here, those in the Extinction Rebellion movement will consider that Taylor is being over-optimistic.

The Danger of Disengaged Subjectivity

As a further point of explanation, Taylor says the pervasive hold instrumental reason has had on modernity is because it employs and promotes an acute form of 'the disengaged model of the human subject' (p. 101), the sense of human being and human thinking 'disengaged' from the dialogical, emotional and traditional 'life forms' (p. 102). This is exemplified by the influence in modernity of mathematical and other forms of calculative reason:

'Arguments, considerations, counsels that can claim to be based on this kind of calculation have great persuasive power in our society, even when this kind of reasoning is not really suited to the subject matter'.

Such reasoning and related applications have influence and high status regardless of its appropriateness to the situations to hand. Taylor, as in Section III, attributes this trend to Cartesian rationalism, arguing that Descartes mistakenly saw the human condition as 'pure mind, distinct from body', and this distorting view of humanity creates much 'regrettable confusion'. It leads to the assumption that we are 'essentially disengaged reason' (p. 103) and that it makes sense to conceive human thinking and selfhood 'on the model of the digital computer'.[1] Taylor, we recall, wants to embrace the capacity of using 'disengaged reason' within the dialogically engaged authenticity of human life, but he does not rate the extreme position that such reasoning can

---

[1] Taylor's thoughts here are taken from his more detailed review on Descartes and the idea of disengaged reason: see *Sources* pp. 143-158.

sometimes have, nor does he favour the reductive view of humans as minds at one remove from the body.

From this, Taylor again seeks a persuasive stance to build towards a restored, balanced outlook. He considers that the cultural and moral background is rich enough to allow a corrective argument to trace genuinely 'moral contexts' within the broader development of instrumental reason. This would involve the following familiar thoughts, reapplied from the earlier developments in the text:

1. The 'sense of ourselves as potentially disengaged reason': as reasoning agents as in the Cartesian model, contains the 'moral ideal, that of a self-responsible, self-controlling reasoning'. There is a rational ideal here of 'autonomous, self-generating thought.' (p. 104)

2. The development of modernity has always had a moral as well as a technological aspect. The moral project was always, Taylor contends, one of improving the wider human condition that individuality is set within.

Building for Retrieval

To support the latter aim of improving the human condition, we sweep back to the seventeenth century and Francis Bacon, whose notion of 'instrumental efficacy' (p. 104) was employed as a criterion of scientific progress.[1] Taylor likes Bacon's view that real progress has been made when a significant difference for the better has been achieved so that change entails relief for 'the condition of mankind'. This therapeutic line of thought has a character that is both 'epistemological', for Bacon championed the experimental, inductive method, and 'moral', as the objective was to improve the human condition. Taylor sees this as having

[1] Francis Bacon (1561-1626): Lawyer, Statesman, scientist and philosopher – his most notable work was *Novum Organum* (1620), which did much to set the tone for the scientific enterprise of modernity.

190

increasing influence as we appreciate the major problems faced in developing nations and see that effective help is simply that which makes a lasting difference.

Here the initiatives in E. F. Schumacher's *Small is Beautiful*, particularly the contrast between advanced and intermediate technology, would illustrate Taylor's point.[1] However, he moves on to confirm how instrumental reason, for all the risks and perils that are entailed, 'has its own rich moral background' (p. 105). The problem is that such reasoning has often been made 'to serve the ends of greater control, of technological mastery'. Structurally, the task of the retrieval of this 'richer moral background' involves showing that the surrender to technological mastery is unnecessary, and this will be, he hopes, in a manner akin to the way in which the ideal of authenticity was rescued from 'the more self-centred modes of self-fulfilment'.

Taylor sets out 'two orders of considerations' for this work of retrieval: these are (a), seeing, against the Cartesian error, the 'ideal of disengaged reason' is simply an ideal – it is not 'a picture of human agency as it really is'. To reiterate, Taylor's point is that the capacity for 'disengaged reason' is set with the life and activity of humans – it is not the encapsulation of the whole meaning of being human. With dialogic notions in mind, Taylor sets out his positive view:

'We are embodied agents, living in dialogical conditions, inhabiting time in a specifically human way, that is, making sense of our lives as a story that connects the past from which we have come to or future projects' (pp. 105-106).

From this, it follows (b) that treating 'a human being'

---

[1] See Schumacher (1974). E. F. Schumacher (1911-1977). Born in Germany, and trained as an economist and statistician, Schumacher came to Britain in the late 1930s and stayed. He worked as Chief Economist to the Coal Board for many years, and developed radical ideas for a plural energy policy and for intermediate technology for development projects.

properly requires that 'we respect this embodied, dialogic temporal nature' (p. 106). The reference to 'respect' here is weighty. It reminds us that the commitment to reciprocal respect between persons is what Taylor's sees as a main, 'ineradicable' theme about human life, as in the point made in *Sources*, that human 'moral instincts' involves the deep sense that 'human life is to be respected'.[1]

To illustrate the significance of this style of respect, Taylor turns to medicine to suggest how over-technological instrumental reason can be countered. In treating patients, medicine cannot work purely on the basis of disengaged neo-Cartesian reason, treating symptoms and conditions with abstract forensic precision. Rather, through rightly motivated professionals, medicine must engage with patients and treat them with respect for their condition – as 'embodied, dialogical, temporal' beings. As Taylor sees it, this means enframing technology within 'an ethic of caring'. This 'enframed technology' is to be set within the 'moral frame of the ethic of practical benevolence', linked to 'a proper understanding of human agency'. The 'proper understanding' Taylor has in mind is the view of dialogic relationality between individuals orientated thereby to the true ideal of creative authenticity. Disengaged reason, which has much that Taylor values, is now retrieved and recast as 'an ideal, rather than as a distorted picture of the human essence' (p. 107).

Taylor thought the work of persuasion and retrieval would be an ongoing struggle over the issues of individualism and the deviant as opposed to the true ideal of authenticity. Similarly, there will be ongoing struggle and debate over the options for this 'enframing' of technology. The framework of disengaged reason and instrumentally driven technology will persist, and the trends to impersonalism will need to be challenged by the framework of 'practical

---

[1] *Sources* p. 8.

benevolence' linked to the life of dialogically related human agents. The struggle here, ongoing like that over the first malaise, takes place in the wider social and political setting, and this brings us to consider the third malaise, the loss of freedom, to which Taylor turns in his final section.

Reading/Revision Questions Section IX *An Iron Cage.*

Makes notes to define, illustrate and explain the following:

1. Which of the three initial 'malaises' of modernity is the focus of this chapter?

2. How do the 'knockers' and 'boosters' differ on the question of technology?

3. How is it that the boosters of self-fulfilment become the knockers of technology and vice versa?

4. How does this contradiction between the 'boosters' and 'knocker' play out with reference to abortion and environmentalism?

5. Why is the dominance of instrumental reason not just a matter of the force of a certain moral outlook?

6. What is the 'iron cage'?

7. Why does Taylor believe that the view of society as an 'iron cage' cannot be sustained?

8. Taylor believes that we are not 'locked in' to a situation we cannot escape. Why?

9. To combat atomism and instrumentalism, what positives does Taylor see in environmentalism?

10. What more do we discover about self-determining freedom in this Section?

11. What error does Descartes make, according to Taylor?

12. What are the three important moral contexts from which the stress on instrumental reason has arisen?

13. Explain what Taylor means with his idea of 'enframing' technology in an 'ethic of practical benevolence'.

11. On 'Against Fragmentation' – Section X[1]

Back to the 'Loss of Freedom'

In the final section of his book, Taylor picks up on the third malaise considered in the first section, and we re-visit the 'loss of freedom' (p. 8f) as related to the culture of dependency that modern society creates through its capacity to fragment human life. The scenario is that as humans, who are naturally social and dialogic, are swept by their own individual enthusiasms into living true to themselves, their interests lead to atomisation and a distortion of the ideal of dialogic authenticity. Given the points made in the previous section, Taylor believes that the pressures of instrumental thinking are great but not so overwhelming that human life is inexorably doomed to be shaped wholly to the constancy of being means to an ever movable end. The solution to this is again to come through a redemptive struggle to retrieve and restore the true ideal of authenticity.

To kick off his review, Taylor considers the role of the institutions of instrumental reason in an ever more technological society. Consistent with his thinking in the previous sections, his view of this is not surprising. He plans to re-enframe such traditions, as we have seen, in 'an ethic of caring' (p. 106) linked to the affirmed 'proper understanding of human agency' where 'agency' evokes the 'dialogic' notion of human life developed earlier in the text – p 32-33). This means that Taylor points up so as to reject alternative proposed solutions that aim to 'leap out of these institutions altogether' (p. 109).

---

[1] The ideas in this section on democratic values and aspirations are also discussed by Taylor in his later essay 'Conditions of an Unforced Consensus on Human Rights'. Taylor (2014) pp. 105-123.

The Danger of Extremes

Drawing again on socio-economic and political history, Taylor once more refers to the then-recent demise of the Soviet Union, and the well-understood economic failures of the collectivist economies of the communist states of Eastern Europe. As Taylor sees things, it seems a truth generally acknowledged that a nation looking for economic stagnation and social decay need look no further than a system of state-controlled collectivism. Such approaches manifest a solution that was no more than a 'dream' (p. 109) of state control managing the economy. However, the collective failure of collectivism and central planning shows how, in marked contrast, modernity confirms that a free-market economy is in some sense 'indispensable' (p.110) for economic success and political, moral and personal freedom. It would, however, be a failure of equal significance if liberal economies were free to operate without any controls or regulations.

Taylor would doubtless think this claim well and truly verified by the financial crisis of 2008, which is generally thought to have come about because of excessive deregulation in the banking and the financial services industry. Taylor's argument is that the demise of the communist economies was due to the failure to control matters with a simple ideal – the communist ideal in this case. He argues, as in his earlier mediation between the 'boosters' and 'knockers' over individualism, that no simple, single principle can work to regulate a complex and fast-moving economy successfully. The 'general will' would fail, as would the wholly free market.

Taylor thinks that a positive social condition might be thought possible if a range of operational factors can be harnessed. He mentions 'market allocations, state planning, collective provision for need, the defence of individual rights, and effective democratic initiative and control'.

196

Taylor here seems to put a high tariff on managing the realties underlying these social and economic factors, suggestive of the position of Keynesian social-democratic political management for modern developed and pluralistic political economies.[1] However, he takes a pragmatic view, suggesting that the short-term effectiveness of any of these five factors could be hampered by any of the others. In the long run, Taylor's thought is that the maximum benefit would come from operating in a balanced way to avoid extremes and manipulations. His view is that 'we can't abolish the market, but nor can we organize ourselves exclusively through markets' (pp. 110-111).

Consistent with his reviews of the earlier malaises, Taylor suggests that there can never be 'a definitive solution' (p. 111) with personal and social life in a political and economic setting of pace and complexity. He sees that there are coexistent trends for fragmentation and atomisation and collaborative and harmonised action. A case in point is how 'the operation of the market and bureaucratic state tends to strengthen the enframings that favour an atomistic and instrumentalist stance to the world and others'. Such institutions 'can never be simply abolished' and so under this liberal ethos, there is ongoing scope for a battle of ideas in the socio-economic setting.

Democratic Hope and the Role of Law

A key agent in the challenge to all the regulations of instrumentalism is the right kinds of democratic institutions. The greatest threat Taylor sees, and which we have indicated to be even more of an issue today, is that the organisational bureaucracy of modernity has substantially weakened the forces of democracy, giving more reason to

---

[1] Reference is made here to the economic theories of John Maynard Keynes (1883-1946), which favoured the use of interventionism to manage national and international economies.

197

the fear of 'tutelary power' (p. 112), attributed again to de Tocqueville, and akin to J. S. Mill's sense of the 'tyranny of the majority' in *On Liberty*.[1] Taylor characterises this as a form of 'soft despotism', but it has the power of fragmenting society and so disabling democratic elements.

What de Tocqueville and Mill develop is a radical challenge to something commonly assumed within democratic thought and experience, that democracy guaranteed intellectual, moral and political freedom. What both appreciated was that this democratic aspiration and ethos inculcates the view that the majority perspective is right and best and that the majority elected to power will act for the general good. These views suppress the freedom of the individual to think and act with critical independence.

Taylor's view is that these negative tendencies lead to people being more inclined to live and think just for themselves, atomistically detached and alienated from participation and engagement with the broader social-political or ethical campaigns. These trends contribute to fragmentation, which Taylor sees as a greater threat than 'despotic control', meaning that people become 'increasingly less capable of forming a common purpose and carrying it out'. This loss of capacity is a symptom of 'the failure of the democratic initiative itself' (p. 113), meaning that atomised individuals are inclined to link to 'common projects with some others' but lose the capacity to have wider 'bonds of sympathy'. All this leads to the troubling view that 'the electorate as a whole is defenceless against the leviathan state'.[2] The outcome is a strengthened view that there is no value or purpose in people trying to pursue their common projects.

Taylor, originally presenting his ideas within and for a

---

[1] See Mill (1987) pp. 63f.
[2] Here Taylor alludes to Thomas Hobbes' *Leviathan* (1651), one of the masterworks of modern political philosophy.

198

Canadian audience, thinks there is particular merit in looking at trends in the near neighbour, the United States of America. There the various negative trends of modernity all have an effect. Within this, one phenomenon of particular note is the increasing use of 'judicial review' (p. 114) to sort out political issues. Judicial review is said to sometimes work to good effect (the *Brown vs the Board of Education* case of 1954, on the desegregation of schools), or it can be altogether more problematic (as in *Roe vs Wade* 1973 – a US Supreme Court ruling that defended the liberty of pregnant women to decide on whether to have an abortion, without excessive government interference). Ideally and so properly, these matters should be resolved within the democratic institution of elective and deliberative assemblies or parliaments.

Taylor thinks the more distinct problem with judicial solutions is that that they are based on a model of problem resolution that entails outcomes that are 'usually winner-take-all' (p. 116). Such an approach might work for many purely legal cases, but in the wider political arena, Taylor thinks more carefully balanced, and inclusive solutions are often required. There are other problems with a reliance on judicial review. It gives undue prominence and status to the legal system and politicises 'the matter of senatorial confirmation of presidential appointments to the Supreme Court' (p. 115).[1]

Taylor then suggests that, as it happens, in the US, there is one strong bastion of defence, namely the legal defence of rights enshrined in the American constitution. Here Taylor is suddenly much more positive about rights than he was earlier in the text.[2] The difference now is that Taylor is endorsing rights that are within the legal framework as

---

[1] Taylor would doubtless see the debates in the USA over President Trump's nominations to the Supreme Court (2017-2020) as an engaging illustration of this process.
[2] See *Authenticity* p. 45 and Chapter 6 above.

opposed to those that are assumed to be inherent in human nature. The Bill of Rights thus provides a rallying point to defend individual and thereby broadly civic values.

Taylor still sees a problem in that the principle of defending individualised rights encourages individuals to collaborate on single-issue campaigns, a very common feature with the American political landscape. The commonality here leads to the problematic 'atrophy' of 'the formation of democratic majorities around meaningful programmes that can be carried to completion'. The 'American political scene' is singled out for criticism, as the political campaigns between the major parties and candidates are so wholly 'disjointed' and 'self-serving'. Doubtless, Taylor would not be encouraged to modify this position by much that he has seen in subsequent American elections.

Further problems remain in developed economies that contribute to the disabling fragmentation referred to above. Atomism and instrumentalism are the outcomes, and Taylor hopes to counter these trends through an appeal to the 'politics of democratic will-formation' (p.118) as a factor in the politics of resistance. Successful common action is key to the generation of a stronger sense of identity within the social bond. The hope is that this builds the will to engage and develop positive and increasingly democratic initiatives, and looking ahead, what this entails is 'a complex and many-levelled struggle, intellectual, spiritual, and political, in which the debates in the public arena interlink with those in a host of institutional' (p. 120).

This ongoing struggle – with *La Lotta Continua* still audible – is to the end of engendering better definitions of the best ways in which the 'enframing technology' and the 'demands of authenticity' and above and beyond these, 'the shape of human life and its relations to the cosmos'.

To move in this direction, we will, Taylor thinks, have to

embrace what is strong and good in modernity so as to face down and defeat what is shallow and weak. The struggle ahead means trying to embrace the '*grandeur*' as well as the '*misère*' (p. 121) of modernity:

'Only a view that embraces both can give us the undistorted insight into our era that we need to rise to its greatest challenge'.

Ongoing acts of participative retrieval to the end of the business of persuasion is the endgame Taylor leaves his readers with, doubtless hoping that his defence of the ideal of authenticity has resonated and persuaded.

Reading/Revision Questions Section *X Against Fragmentation.*

Makes notes to define, illustrate and explain the following:

1. According to Taylor, why did classical Marxism and Leninism collapse?

2. Why can there never be, according to Taylor, a definitive solution to the problems posed by market efficiency within the modern welfare state?

3. What does Taylor mean by 'fragmentation'? Why does it pose more of a danger for our society than does the loss of freedom of soft despotism?

4. According to Taylor, why and how does fragmentation come about?

5. In this new fragmented situation, Taylor thinks two facets of political life take on greater and greater 'saliency': explain, illustrate and assess this pair of 'facets'.

6. What problems does Taylor see with democracy?

7. According to Taylor, how has Canada been more fortunate than the United States concerning the question of fragmentation?

8. What does Taylor portray as the situation we face as he concludes his book? How accurate is his prognosis, given that he wrote this in 1991?

12. Assessing Taylor's Work of Retrieval

We have now worked over the presentation of ideas that Taylor sets out in his text. We have seen the problems he identifies and the various lines of discussion he generates to the end of finding a solution in terms of a definition and defence of the ethics of authenticity. We have noted his positive and critical explanations and suggestions for what he favours and what is against and commented on some of the issues arising. We have delved into some of the lines of criticism to which Taylor might be open, and in this chapter, we will draw together and review some of the problems surrounding Taylor's case. As we shall see, there are some points we pick up from some of the matters discussed earlier, and some of the issues we now consider will overlap, this in consequence of the style of philosophical anthropology employed by Taylor. Just as Taylor sought an exercise in retrieval to recover the ethical ideal of authenticity, we need to retrieve the components in his presentation of the emergent ethics of authenticity.

The Puzzle of the 'Ethics of Authenticity.'

Early on, we identified some questions raised by Taylor's project of defending an ethic of authenticity. We noted that if the moral ideals in question have to do with 'being true to oneself' (p. 15) and living toward ideals of a 'better' (p. 16) or 'higher' mode of life, then we need to know what was meant by 'better', 'higher' and 'being true to oneself'. In thinking about how these values would be defined, further points came up; we wondered whether the idea would be that the values in question were seen as in some way intrinsic to the human condition or as preferred qualities acquired through life. We also raised some issues about how an ethic might relate to morality, to the metaethical concern and to how the form and content of the ethic of authenticity would appear.

As it turns out, the exposition of the ethics of authenticity is a soft-focus, gradualist affair. Perhaps this is no surprise given Taylor's self-understanding of operating to develop work in the style of philosophical anthropology as distinct from something slotted into the framework of conventional moral philosophy.[1] Taylor indicates that in the text, as in the original lectures, he is constrained by a lack of 'space' (p. 12). Doubtless this has something to do with what then unfolds. We find that Taylor moves along section by section with ideas that are asserted, drawn in and evolved. He makes some references and allusions and gradually builds up the composite that makes up the identikit picture of the ethical ideal of authenticity. Working out what this amounts to as a guide to human life, which is what is usually provided by an ethic is, to modify an earlier illustration, a bit like unpacking a piece of self-assembly furniture and finding that there are, as a guide only schematic instructions written in an alien language. To build, we need to lay all the parts out and see if we can work out where and how the various bits connect. Similarly, to make sense of what we have found with the material presented by Taylor, we need to pull together the elements and offer a summary presentation of what he seems to be arguing. In so doing, we can assess whether we have the components giving the form and content of an ethic as a reasoned guide for the business of life or something rather different.

Looking over Taylor's book, the ideal of authenticity he is keen on has to do with the capacity human individuals have for creative self-affirmation to the end that they discover and become more fully themselves. The stress in the idea for this is that the proper ideal of authenticity entails the individual living so as to fuse autonomous self-discovery within conscious and collaborative relations with the wider community and its history and culture, including the vital

---

[1] See Chapter 1 above.

backdrop of inescapably significant 'horizons' (p. 37). In effect, this is the setting for the 'moral ontology' to which Taylor refers in *Sources*.[1] He is keen on seeing that properly understood, the ethic of authenticity marries the life of the individual with the history, thought, culture and life of the community. This is related to the idea that humans live embedded in the complex of these structures and traditions, and so this, Taylor thinks, gives a variegated rather than uniform moral texture to the human condition. This means that the values Taylor has in mind, of living towards ways that are 'better' and 'higher', while also 'being true to the self', are all based on capacities nurtured in the communal and dialogic setting of human life. These capacities are givens of the human condition, but the expertise in deploying them are cultivated in and through the processes of living. All of this is a part of the project of developing the philosophical anthropology favoured by Taylor.[2] He sets out his position as a counter to the 'worry' of 'individualism' (p. 2), where individualism is seen as an end in itself, as he discusses it as one of the three 'malaises' (p. 1).

One implication of this approach is that Taylor avoids employing either of the ways of dealing with the relationship between morality and ethics that we explained earlier.[3] Taylor does not seem to see morality and ethics as interchangeable: instead, he sees the moral dimension of life as bounded in with life, but insofar as we cultivate 'higher' and 'better' stands of value, we can articulate an ethical expression of this as a mode of being. However, we do not find Taylor racing to market anything he has produced in the usual package of a normative ethic. Insofar as real life is what Taylor wants to focus on, with the patterns of dialogic relations, history and culture, moral philosophy in its conventional arrays would seem so much artifice.

---

[1] See *Sources* pp. 3-24.
[2] Again, see Chapter 1 above.
[3] See the Introduction above.

Another thing that Taylor shows great self-restraint on is becoming prescriptive, of putting a system of rules and precepts into the outline of the ethics of authenticity. In a later essay, 'Perils of Moralism', he writes of his unease at the 'code-fetishism' that pervades modernity, of how much effort is invested in the 'modern liberal society' - which is still fragmented and atomised – to engage in 'defining and applying codes of conduct'.[1] In social and everyday life, it is common to find sets of codes and rules being drawn up and regularised for every new twist and turn in life where this or that interest group promotes a cause and reasons why something needs a new set of protective rules. This is achieved due to 'the legal entrenchment of certain fundamental principles in our society, whose most prominent and visible form is the institutionalization of various charters of rights and nondiscrimination, which is a central feature of this world.'

The problem is that this gives rise to a complex of 'legally binding codes' which are assumed to be the right and proper way 'to achieve certain important collective goods'.[2] Here Taylor has in mind codes on aspects of equality such as mutual respect and tolerance and matters to do with eliminating offences against others through 'speech codes', and there are doubtless more recent codes to protect gender assignation rights, pronoun usage and so on. Taylor is concerned that with the 'code fetish', we have rather instrumental means to achieve very limited benefits, with the deeper, richer insights that are possible for human life being obscured. In *Sources*, *Authenticity* and again in the 'Perils of Moralism', Taylor opposed narrow, prescriptive codification because of the restrictive entailments of such an approach in the face of both changing circumstances and the multiple or plural goods that are evident within the tradition. The whole point is that these goods coexist, even

---

[1] 'Perils of Moralism' in Taylor (2014) p. 347.
[2] Taylor (2014) p. 348.

though they may sometimes come into tension or conflict – as in the case of 'liberty and equality; commutative justice and comity; efficient success and compassionate understanding; getting things done bureaucratically (requiring categories, rules) and treating everyone as a unique person; and so on'.

Taylor argues that the phenomenon of rule-governance goes back to the puritan age and that the consequent reaction, moving on to the period of Romanticism, such as he reviews in *Authenticity*, is where we find the resurgence of variety, individualism and pluralism.[1] Taylor, unsurprisingly, is not eager to renege on this and adopt a rule-governed mode of life.

In modernity, another point we have seen Taylor notes is that a key feature is that 'people are no longer sacrificed to the demands of supposedly sacred orders that transcend them' (p. 2). The modern conception of human freedom is one of individuals 'breaking loose from older moral horizons' (p. 3) that involved a 'larger order'. Following Bloom, Taylor presses forward with the view that in a 'flattened' and 'narrowed' (p. 4) form, self-orientated individualism comes about, and this, with the input of instrumental reason, leads to people being fragmented and atomised. We are left with a diminished and distorted mode of authentic being, a distortion of the ideal to which Taylor's text offers 'persuasion' (p. 72) toward a form of 'retrieval' (p. 80).

Taylor's notion of the true, authentic self involves the view that the self's development and fulfilment has a dual need for both individuality and community. Social rituals and norms thus have more than an instrumental purpose. Discrediting these rituals is described as 'disenchantment'

---

[1] See Taylor (2014) p. 353f and *Authenticity* Section III pp. 25-29.

(p. 3), implying a loss of magic, mystery and vision in the human condition.[1] The loss of community entailed leads to 'fragmentation' (p. 112), and the development of a condition where people are increasingly less capable of forming a common purpose and carrying it out; fragmentation occurs as a consequence of the trend of atomism, as people increasingly do their own thing, and relations of kinship and common interests with fellow citizens deteriorate.

We saw how Taylor argues that amongst the losses suffered by humanity in modernity, there is a loss of a 'heroic dimension' (p. 4) where there is a lack of a higher purpose or cause worth dying for and a loss of passion. Instead, there is a growth of the 'politics of equal recognition' (p. 49), giving a pluralistic notion of the political condition, with competing campaigns for particular causes of singular intent, such as nationalism, ethnic politics, feminism, multiculturalism and the environment.

Given that pluralism risks adding to fragmentation, Taylor wants to counter the negative trends, and we have seen he rests a lot of his case on the affirmation of mutual respect between persons.[2] This is linked to promoting Taylor's signature idea of human life being '*dialogical*' (p. 33) and socially engaged, not simply as a centre of subjective self-consciousness. Taylor also suggests a tension whereby humans are aware of a basic limitation of capacity for understanding by the cultural frameworks that make our individuality and understanding possible, yet are also opened up for positive change through dialogic communicative relationships.[3] In this more positive mode, 'our understanding of the good things in life can be transformed by our enjoying them in common with people

---

[1] Taylor takes this notion of 'disenchantment' from Weber – see *Sources* p. 186.

[2] See *Sources* p. 9 and *Authenticity* p. 77.

[3] See *Authenticity* pp. 63-66 and Chapter 7 above.

we love' (p. 34). Taylor adds that 'some goods become accessible to us only through such common enjoyment'. These affirmations are to live in a relational manner of association with others and against the risks of slipping into over-subjective deviations. Living this tension but getting to the condition of operating as a dialogic individual is to operate with the true ethical ideal of authenticity.

What we can see from this summary is that Taylor constructs in phases what we can term a phenomenological perspective on the dynamic, dialogic, and so creative and referential form of life that fits the brief for the ethic of authenticity. What Taylor sets out to avoid, and we can see that to the end of his book, he has successfully avoided it, is the customary route that ethicists are inclined to follow. As we have mentioned before, in the narrative history of the study and development of ethics, it is customary to either conduct a careful analysis of moral terms so as to establish their cognitive status, their sense and meaning, and so their viability in discourse, or to build from some such opening analyses, a developed proposal of a normative ethic. G. E. Moore's *Principia Ethica* is a classic example emphasising the first approach, which we now call 'metaethics'; Alasdair MacIntyre's *Against Virtue* is an influential example of the second approach.

Taylor scrupulously avoids both of these operational styles. If we recall Taylor's autobiographical piece consulted in our opening chapter, we can see that although his book is presented as '*The Ethics of Authenticity*', for reasons that go back to his student days at Oxford, he does not engage in a metaethical audit of the core terms he is going to count as significant, showing along the way how significance is to be warranted; as we have seen, he does not give all that much by way of developed detail for the justified normative 'ethic of authenticity' to show how it provides the *modus operandi* for an ethical life. Taylor is emphatic in rejecting these trends in ethics as misguided.[1] He is truer to the method and scheme of a broader approach of human and philosophical reflection, and unlike a substantial wedge of modern philosophers, he thinks history, and the history of culture, have a great deal to do with our understanding of the human condition. This means that by the conventions of academic philosophy, *Authenticity* is unusual. To coin a phrase, it enframes a good deal, but the focus is on historical, cultural and philosophical explanation rather than on pages of tight deductive reasoning. Thus the exposition comes in waves of explanation and in the manner of 'persuasion' (p. 72) rather than hard reasoning.

The puzzle alluded to in the title of this section is that through the phases of *Authenticity*, Taylor builds up the case, not so much for a normative ethic but for a way of reading the human condition as an ethically resonant state of dialogic being. By the subtle process of explanation, Taylor redraws the map of ethical understanding to show that the base datum for reflection is the human condition in all of its richness and manifold variation. Students reading *Authenticity* often comment that the book feels like a combination of cultural history and creative philosophical reflection, which given Taylor's focus, is a pretty accurate response. The underlying point here is that had the title *The Malaise of Modernity* been retained throughout, the tensions here would be much reduced.

Taylor's preferred approach involves writing descriptively to explain and contrast trends in social and intellectual life, affirming certain lines of development as having status or significance, working more as a social or historical theorist describing the data set than as a philosopher defining and defending a case. To a greater rather than a lesser extent, he operates with a soft form of moral realism, using or alluding to concepts such as respect 'for the background of things

---

[1] For detail here see *Sources*, especially Part 1.

that matter' (p. 40) and 'responsibilization' (p. 77) as if what they mean is more or less self-evident.

We come back to the points in the earlier part of his presentation, where Taylor sketches the outline of 'a picture of what a higher or better mode of life would be, where "better" or "higher" are defined not in terms of what we happen to desire or need, but offer a standard of what we ought to desire' (p. 16). Here, and on several other occasions, Taylor refers to notions of obligation, alluding to something prior or higher.[1] The 'inescapable horizons' (pp. 31ff) come into view soon after. We have also seen that Taylor refers to commitments that are other than purely individual and subjective as having greater worth for truly enabling the realisation of the ethic of authenticity. His idea is simply that to be a truly authentic individual, a person comes to be in and through relationships with, following Mead, 'significant others' (p. 33). This relates to his view that an authentically ethical person is evident, in Taylor's analysis, as he moves to his view that the fundamental quality of human life is manifest through its '*dialogical* character' (p. 33). We have suggested that with this notion, Taylor links up with a clear tradition in contemporary thought that sees cultural and social life providing the setting and general preconditions for personal being. Thus we are all born into and grow within a culture where we acquire 'languages of expression' by processes of induction through dialogue with others who are prior. It is through 'exchanges with others' that individuals gain the means to be self-developers, and this reveals that there is always a backdrop and point of reference for that individualisation. Taylor's view is that we continue to operate in the tension of dialogue with others to express, explain, and justify our individuality and the orientation of our self-determined perspectives.

---

[1] See *Authenticity* pp. 5, 8 and 44.

If we put these components of thought together, we see that the 'ethic of authenticity' is actualised as within and from our dialogic setting, we cultivate 'the moral ideal behind self-fulfilment' by being 'true to oneself' (p. 15). The 'moral ideal' here draws on the 'principle of originality' (p. 29). In this, and in contemporary experience as Taylor portrays it, authenticity is linked to 'the individualism of self-fulfilment' (p. 14). However, the 'moral ideal' (p. 16) envisaged is not achieved through a route of purely individualised interests, with the attendant dangers of subjectivism and 'the culture of narcissism' (p. 57): it comes through the use of a version of 'disengaged rationality' (p. 25) that provides the capacity for evaluative reflection, again, as set within the organic complex of dialogic life, Taylor claims that individual human identity 'crucially depends on... dialogical relations with others' (p. 48).

By these interactive means, we cultivate a resurgence of 'responsibilization' (p. 77) and, guided by 'intersubjective justice' (p. 66), move to a form of positive activism within a democratic society. We bond in reciprocal relations of mutual respect for others and the wider reality, not least the environment, through a deliberate policy of 'enframing' activities with 'the ethic of practical benevolence' (p. 106).

Central to this whole outlook is Taylor's affirmation that the 'moral ideal behind self-fulfilment is that of being true to oneself' (p. 15), and whilst this would seem to be grounded in potentialities that are given with being human, we saw that Taylor wisely sees the pursuit of the ideal in the collaborative relations of dialogic life: he also envisages the pursuit as developing within the context of 'living a whole life' (p. 53).

This theme can be linked to the view in *Sources* that 'to understand our moral world we have to see what ideas and pictures underlie our sense of respect for others and those which underpin our notions of a full life'.[1] With these time extended perspectives of his thought in place, Taylor might work up a more elaborate dialogic ethic of interpersonalism, on the basis that interpersonal life is the basis of the greater social whole; his references to obligation and to that which is 'better' could be unpacked to relate, as a neo-Kantian might, to the imperative of treating others as persons, as ends and never as means only, making this an operational principle for the anti-instrumentalist ethic of authenticity. However, despite the high tariff he places on dignity, Taylor does not move far in this direction, affirming the indelible weight of respect for responsibility and respect for persons, but leaving the specifics of what he insistently calls 'the ethics' of authenticity as something we have to estimate more from the patterns suggested by various affirmations than from what else is said.[2]

All of this is consistent with the style of Taylor's project with *Authenticity*. He elaborates an ethical perspective from and for the human condition, rather than a detailed set of precepts for everyday life. For the reasons considered earlier, Taylor is not in the least over-prescriptive, generating no sets of obligations or duties for responsive and responsible living. He offers perspectives expressive of aspiration or hope but expressed descriptively and through explanatory reason rather than argumentative force. For one keen to construct a 'work of retrieval' (p. 23) and a 'work of persuasion' (p. 72), this could be seen as something of a weakness. And indeed, it would be if Taylor were aiming to elaborate and sell a specific theory or ideology, but his view is different: humanity has, he thinks, to a worrying extent, lost the plot by buying into theoretical or ideological solutions.[3] The better way, Taylor thinks, is to look at life, the human condition, and reset the way we live now in light of the richness in the tradition.

---

[1] *Sources* p. 14.

[2] For Taylor on dignity see *Sources* p. 15f

[3] See Taylor on Marxism – *Authenticity* p. 109

Taylor's rationale for this is linked to his multiple references to artistic and moral creativity and to the component of the ideal of authenticity that carries the greatest hope as well as the greatest risk. We are individuals, and unless we embrace the creative challenge of thinking, feeling and acting on our own initiative, we will betray the ideal of authenticity. We can act with initiative and creativity, referencing the 'inescapable horizons' (p. 37), especially those involving dialogic relations, but we cannot live the authentic ideal sitting perennially on the fence.

As we mentioned earlier when considering Trilling, the idea of being true to oneself has a strong Shakespearean ring to it, as in Polonius' advice to his son Laertes, which puts 'above all' the principle of being true 'to thine own self' to guarantee that 'thou canst not then be false to any man'.[1] Polonius' meaning, with which this advice concludes, has to do with a person having discretion, self-respect, values of integrity and honour, and an implicit bond of equal regard for those who are likewise disposed. The ideas floated here by Shakespeare echo classical notions of acting with what we might term character and in accordance with virtue.

As we have seen, with *Authenticity*, Taylor is highly reticent in his attitude to contemporary modes of virtue ethics. This leads to his concept of authenticity being oddly dislocated from a strong element in a tradition where 'authenticity' has resonance.[2] Cultivating the critique that a virtue ethicist might make of Taylor would be one excellent topic for a further philosophic excursion. However, there is another matter that Taylor might have picked up more on, namely, the currency of the theme of authenticity in existential thought, an expressive tradition of continental thought that he certainly appreciates. Given the other things he alludes to, it is perhaps surprising that Taylor does not do this.

---

[1] See Chapter 3 above.
[2] See *Authenticity* p. 19.

214

Authenticity and Existentialism

Existentialism is a philosophical approach that has had an ongoing influence from the 1930s to the present. Popularised variants of this style of philosophy embedded in public consciousness resurface as people express a sense of 'existential threats' to life as we know it. This might be from commentators and activists for Extinction Rebellion or from those worrying about the Covid19 Pandemic, but there are many other threats and issues considered to manifest an existential challenge to the value and purpose of human life.[1]

In Taylor's *Sources,* it is obvious from the references to Heidegger that existential thinking is not placed into the deviant form of the ideal of authenticity, where the over-individualised, over-subjective, and somewhat narcissistic variants are in evidence.[2] Taylor's references show that existential and phenomenological thinking affirms a positive subjectivity against over-mechanical views of reality prompted by instrumentalism, science and technology.[3] What is clear is that in philosophical forms, the existential style promotes authentic life as featuring a combination of courage and realism to accept a view of life grounded in the awareness of limitation, of finitude, and so conditioned by the horizon of time. This is the core tension explored in Heidegger's *Being and Time*. Existential authenticity also entails capacities for self-awareness, choice, and commitment within the interpersonal or dialogic sphere. Regardless of Taylor's avoidance of existentialism in his development of *Authenticity*, it is worth

---

[1] The idea of citing some examples here is rather blown by the sheer number appearing from one internet search: existential threats to human life from Nanotechnology, Super Intelligent computers, existential threats to the BBC (funding issues), Freedom – due to Covid and 'woke' issues – and many others all indicative of a challenge to human self-understanding and value.

[2] See *Sources* p. 257.

[3] See *Sources* pp. 460-463 and pp. 481-482.

exploring the existential perspective to see what might be available here for a renewed ethic of authenticity.

Existential writers have many distinct interests, but one thing that is held in common is an attitude of anti-essentialism, the view that there are no fixed, determining, *a priori* values or essences in virtue of which individual life is set. These are all, against Taylor, escapable horizons, and the alternative existentialist maxim from Sartre is that 'existence precedes essence'.[1] Sartre's vision is far from unproblematic, but we can retrace the position he sketches.

In his writings, in *Being and Nothingness* (1943) and in *Existentialism and Humanism* (1945), Sartre uses explicitly and sometimes implicitly ideas of a two-aspect view, involving the *'en-soi'* and the *'pour-soi'*.[2] This is, in effect, a form of ontic dualism: physical objects, including the human body, are said to exist in a style or mode that is best-termed existence *en-soi,* or existence 'in-itself'. Whether natural or manufactured, physical objects are what they are; moreover, they exist in such a way that they cannot be other than what or how they are. Things in the category of the 'in-itself' are set within and determined by a pattern of structural and causal laws and conditions. In contrast, and in virtue of their facility for self-consciousness, humans have as a possibility that mode or style of existence best-termed existence *pour-soi*, or existence 'for-itself'. There is, Sartre thinks, a dramatic tension for the being existing 'for-itself'. This tension arises because the self-conscious mode of being is literally set within the physical mode of biological existence, which falls into the 'in-itself' category.

With these points, we find a rootedness in subjectivity in Sartre that has more than a hint of affinity with Taylor's

---

[1] Sartre (1980) p. 28. J-P Sartre (1905-1980). Sartre's *Existentialism and Humanism* was originally given as a public lecture in Paris in 1945. The original title of the lecture is 'Existentialism is a Humanism'.
[2] See *Authenticity* p. 16.

teaching on the importance of being true to oneself, and, as we have seen, Taylor traces this to the moves with rationality made by Descartes. Similarly, Sartre sources the capacity for self-conscious rationality by references to Descartes, and when he uses the 'essence' versus 'existence' distinction, he articulates a sense of the *en soi/pour soi* distinction. In Sartre's presentation, it is illustrated by reference to items of manufacture, things for which it is appropriate to claim that their essence precedes their existence.

Sartre's key example is of a paper knife and its manufacture.[1] His idea is that such knives are produced by people who have preconceptions of the nature, form, dimensions, style and function of the knife and further knowledge of the method of manufacture by means of which the knife will come into being. Before the paper knife's existence, the people who make it know what it is, how to produce it, and its purpose. Accordingly, Sartre says of the paper knife 'that its essence – that is to say the sum of the formulae and the qualities which made its production and definition possible – precedes its existence.' Sartre's view is that we are taking a 'technical standpoint' in our view of things.[2]

Sartre considers that the theological view of the world works in much the same way. God is the 'supernal artisan', and the creation stands as the consequence and expression

---

[1] By a paper knife Sartre means a letter opener, not uncommon in homes and offices in the times when letters were a main form of communication.

[2] Sartre (1980 p. 27. If we take another example, a person's leg as a part of the body exists in the mode of the *en soi*. That person's mind and self-consciousness operate in the mode of existence *pour soi*. If we imagine that one of the person's legs is amputated for good medical reasons, the now-amputated leg is even more distinctly a part of existence *en-soi*. The one-legged person is still a person who, as a person, can operate in the mode of existing *pour-soi*. However, a person who is very drunk or overdosed on some recreational drug will not, for some time, escape existence *en soi*.

of the divine will. Thus, 'the conception of man in the mind of God is comparable to that of the paper-knife in the mind of the artisan.' Both work to a product through a process based on a formula or conception. Sartre thinks a similar habit of mind can be found in the atheistic philosophy of the Enlightenment, where various theories offered variations on the theme of all humans possessing a basic 'human nature', of all humans being exemplars of this common nature in virtue of which they are human. Again, an essence or ideal of humanity precedes existence. Contrary to this, Sartre explicitly operates as an atheistic existentialist, claiming that if there is no God, and if ideological theories also fail, then there is one being whose existence precedes his essence, a 'being which exists before it can be defined by any conception of it.'[1] That 'being' is man, or, as Sartre suggests, referencing Heidegger, 'the human reality'.

The existential outlook has definite implications for the treatment Sartre gives to the interpersonal sphere of activity, where humans have the arresting capacity to operate in either mode of being: the other may be seen as an object 'in-itself' in the world or as a subjective and free agent existing 'for-itself'. One might say that humans can operate so that they objectify others, see them as things, use and abuse them, and treat them instrumentally, so regarding them in a manner of which Taylor would certainly disapprove. Alternatively, humans can operate seeing the other as another free individual and so enter into dialogic and relational exchanges, which Taylor would endorse.

Sartre is eager to press a positive estimate of his approach to existentialism against a range of criticisms that suggest it provides negative, over-romantic and anti-social perspectives on life. Sartre refutes the charge, claiming that existentialism offers a truly optimistic doctrine since it 'confronts man with the possibility of choice'.[2] His view is

[1] Sartre (1980) p. 28
[2] Sartre (1980) p. 25.

that rightly understood, existentialism entails the 'least scandalous and most austere' of teachings; this is because what all genuine existentialists have in common is the view that 'existence comes before essence - or, if you will, that we must begin from the subjective'.[1]

It might be thought that Sartre's existentialism is highly individualised. It is certainly disparaging about the status and legitimacy of *a priori* concepts, essences, ideals or natures concerning human experience. Sartre affirms that the fundamental premise for thought is existence or being. He thinks that if there is no *a priori* essence of humanity, there is no goal, destiny, purpose, meaning or value to history. In this perspective, authentic meaning, value, and purpose come into being relative to the individual's active existential choices and affirmations. In a sense, Sartre's existentialism is as anti-ideological as Taylor's dialogic view of humanity. For Sartre, there are no hard, objective absolutes residing in and as the essence of things upon which we can thus rely for the life we lead. Sartre's view of the character of reality is that it is fluid and plastic. Full, proper and authentic existence is thus relative to the extent to which a person lives a life that expresses his own choices and determinations.

There is an affinity between Sartre and Taylor in that both defend a form of expressive and value-creating choice. Taylor is keen on defending 'self-determining freedom' (p. 27) in the context of the individual deciding 'for themselves alone'. However, this decision-making is set with and against the backdrop of a layer of horizons 'of issues of importance' (p. 39). In contrast, Sartre might be thought to be affirming the horizon-lite view that the validation of individuality comes through self-affirmation alone, but in fact, he is clear in rejecting any suggestion that his existential doctrine entails an overly individualised, narrow

---

[1] Sartre (1980) p. 26.

or diminished view of what it is to be human. Sartre's idea is that in his understanding, existentialism is a doctrine 'that does render human life possible'. Crucially he adds that 'every truth and every action imply both an environment and a human subjectivity'.[1] He means that the human situation is always one of encounter, not just with the impersonal aspects of the external world, but with other individuals whose existence and reality confronts us. Sartre's exposition references the wider culture in a far less detailed way than Taylor, but historical mindfulness should help us here: at the time of writing – the mid-1940s – Sartre was busily engaged, not just with his existential thinking; he was writing reviews, plays and novels as embedded in the cultural scene as it is possible to be. The point is, this would be well-known to the audience for whom he was presenting his existential message.

Like Taylor, Sartre wants to restore and promote the dignity and responsibility that comes with being human. In Sartre's presentation, his view is that humans validate their life and achieve purpose through their own actualised choices. In the settings of life, they do this in relation to others, but the primary responsibility lies with the individual. This means that the existentialist affirmation simply asserts that man is of 'greater dignity than a stone or table'. He continues:

'For we mean to say that man primarily exists – that man is, before all else, something which propels itself before a future and is aware that it is doing so. Man is, indeed, a project which possesses a subjective life, instead of being a kind of moss, or a fungus or a cauliflower. Before that projection of the self nothing exists; not even in the heaven of intelligence: man will only attain existence when he is what he purposes to be'.

The existentialist affirms that as existence is and remains prior to essence, man is 'responsible for what he is.' Existentialism thus puts man 'in possession of himself as he

---

[1] Sartre (1980) p. 24.

is'; it puts 'the entire responsibility for his existence squarely upon his own shoulders.'

This outline of Sartre's notions, which includes a neat variant of self-determining freedom, suggests that existential authenticity provides a centred ethical orientation that offers a clean and direct rationale for authentic life that compliments the aspiration with an antecedent perspective from which Taylor could benefit.

A difference between Sartre and Taylor is that while Taylor wants to ally authentic choosing to a rich layer of horizons of meaning, Sartre is far less explicit about this and does not attempt to orientate the existential pattern of authentication to wider generalised horizons of meaning, such as Taylor likes. On this point, there is a clear reason why Taylor would not allude to or draw on this line of thought. This avoidance is unfortunate in the sense that existentialism, as Sartre expresses it in his novels and plays and philosophical writings, is engaged with the political circumstances of life, and it certainly does not promote the detached atomistic approach of which Taylor is so critical. Existential thinking is also strongly based in the intersubjectivity of 'dialogic' human relations, and it offers some positive resources that would energise and enhance Taylor's case and make for a more richly resourced defence of his ethic of authenticity.

The Problems of 'Horizons of Significance'

Taylor argues that authenticity requires not simply that individuals have choices to unfold their sense of self-identity. They must also operate with reference to 'horizons of significance' (p. 39). By 'horizons of significance', Taylor means those traditions, values, principles, concepts or ideals within the background tradition and culture that provide means by which we are able to interpret and make sense of real-life situations, whether personal, interpersonal, social, or cultural. We might as horizons include the past, the duties of being a citizen and of being a person in solidarity with others, and the needs of the environment.[1] Such horizons give setting, context, background, and a frame of reference, so make more manageable and more meaningful the moral choices that we make. Through choices orientated to the horizons, we avoid the trend Taylor consistently argues against of falling into subjectivity, narcissism, and moral relativism.

We have already reviewed Taylor's 'inescapable horizons' in our discussion of Section IV.[2] We now need to pull together some points of criticism to review this notion and assess how it is defended.

We consider first some of the typical concerns arising for student readers of Taylor's text.[3] One issue often raised is that for a work looking at the problems of modernity, the way Taylor references the horizons is somewhat conservative, sometimes nostalgic, perhaps even reactionary. Taylor writes evocatively of life in simpler times, with less technology and allegiances to levels of reality and 'Great chains of being' (p. 3). From this, there is a sense that too much of modernity is vulnerable to being devalued. Referential horizons can sound helpful, and, to repeat a point, if we live in Canadian society (whether in 1991 or 2021), where a range of agreeable horizonal demands to do with society, nature, history, and so on might not seem hard to find, we can see what Taylor means. But the wider problem is that if we were in a setting akin to Germany under National Socialism or Syria in 2021, we are likely to be confronted with highly ambiguous horizons, many of which are unlikely to be appealing for the development of authenticity. Taking the historical example of Germany, from all that has emerged in the years since

---

[1] See *Authenticity* p. 22
[2] See Chapter 5 above.
[3] Here I draw on recollections from my I.B. Philosophy classes.

1945, it seems that it was extremely hard for many Germans living under National Socialism to penetrate to deeper, more enlightened horizons.[1] All-round, this makes the appeal of horizons problematic. As amelioration, Taylor's axiomatic referencing of the human possession of an 'ineradicable sense that human life is to be respected' is very helpful, as is his affirmation against the tyrannies and dictatorships.[2] However, in *Authenticity*, Taylor mainly uses historical and anthropological explanations to ground the ideas he finds more persuasive, leaving the feeling that his ideas need greater clarity and support.

Taylor's problem can be re-expressed through the contrast between, on the one hand, his celebration of the plurality of the modern world, and on the other, his argument against some versions of authenticity – those versions that stress individualism in the way that entails an emphasis on subjectivity and relativism. This is another worry for some readers of his text, who, as Bloom might have predicted, think there is a case for a clear place for subjectivity and relativism. Taylor is, as ever, looking to achieve a restorative balance, but, arguably, he works so as to entail a risk of inconsistency, as subjectivity and relativism are aspects of the contemporary cultural 'horizon'; they are components in the plurality. The worry for Taylor's project is that he wants to defend what he says is the true ideal of authenticity, so rescuing it from the 'travestied' form, but the persistent question is that of whether such an evolution in the ideal is in the nature of the ideal itself. If 'being true to oneself' is at the heart of authenticity as Taylor presents it, it is hard to see how to rule out altogether distinct strands of individualism, subjectivism and relativity.

Taylor resists this criticism and wants to incorporate these strands of individualism within the rebranded ethic of authenticity, as components within dialogic relations and as

---

[1] On this see Burleigh (2000).
[2] *Sources* p. 8.

a part of a creative life in relation to horizons of significance. In part, he tries to build this up by an appeal to certain traditions and values as relevant, so we have the notion of a 'background of intelligibility' (p. 37) and the suggestion of 'a horizon of important questions' (p. 40) within which individuals define themselves 'meaningfully'. However, when Taylor affirms the horizons provided by 'the demands of society, or nature… history and the bonds of solidarity', we receive a provocative list. If we consider simply the broadly Western tradition on which Taylor mostly draws, what 'society', 'nature', 'history' and the 'bonds of society' cumulatively entail amounts to a very considerable and far from uniform sum total of variable influence. Taylor clearly thinks that residual human interests in terms of an ethical outlook of care and concern for the well-being of others gives a kind of thread upon which the garments of authentic life can be spun, but for all that, the issue that remains troubling is that the appeal to the 'horizons of significance' seems highly generalised.

On the matter of the shape and content of the range of 'demands' made by 'society', 'nature' and 'history', we get little by way of guidance. Crucial for Taylor is the point that individuals personally come to terms with the understanding that '*independent of*' the will, 'there is something noble, courageous, and hence significant in giving shape to my own life' (p. 39). 'Something', but on the face of it, we are not given elaborate referencing as to what, bar from the other components in the package of ideas Taylor provides. This means we are left with the thought that there is a 'something', but it is not clear what, that, independent of anyone's will, has the weight and power to give 'shape' to individuality. As we have seen, this can be seen as a challenge to the integrity of the freedom that the ethics of authenticity was largely supposed to defend.[1]

---

[1] See Chapter 5 above.

Taylor has two particular lines of thought that explain and serve to defend his view. One evident in many of his reflections is the idea that free choice and action do not happen in a vacuum. Our lives make sense and can be rendered meaningful not through singular or 'monological' (p. 33) but 'dialogical' commitments. In defending this, Taylor is consistent in avoiding extremes. He does not think that in the dealings of human life, choice and activity are wholly shrouded by determinism; nor do humans have absolute freedom; instead, humans have the capacity for 'self-responsible freedom.'[1] This has an operational range within a setting; it does not empower or justify absolute liberty. Taylor's view is, perhaps, akin to the situation of people in a restaurant: they are free over what they choose, but they have to choose from what is on offer, whether from the menu or, through dialogic exchange and negotiation with the chef over what can be produced as a special. People are also free to leave the restaurant, and as in a restaurant, so in life, we are free to live in relativism, subjectivism and monological narcissism. Taylor's thought is that we are not obliged to choose this and that it is better if we do not so choose.

The second line of explanation that defends Taylor's use of horizons of significance is to do with his sense of his project as one of retrieval. He is retrieving the principle of self-identity being forged through the process of choice, by individual decision-making. This is a factor in why he is persistently agnostic about being prescriptive over how we should live. He is aiming to rescue and redeem individualism from self-indulgent extremes and narcissistic tendencies. One point he makes about the referencing of horizons of significance that we must not underplay is that he mentions that the mix, range and variety in the said horizons reveal complexity and a range of ideas, which show how and why 'some things are worthwhile, and others

[1] *Sources* p. 407.

less so, and still others not at all' (p. 38). Earlier, we termed this his 'the good, the bad and the ugly' point about horizons, and it reminds us that Taylor is alert to the instructional value of tradition and that the instructional value is shaped to the contours of human life, so what is on offer is guidance on what might and what will not work well in the ongoing routine and drama of life. Taylor assumes that our capacity for disengaged reason and care will empower discernment in both learning from the horizons and choosing how to act with reference to what is best going forward in the ongoing struggle over the business of life.

This means that we can recalibrate the problem we have raised over establishing the moral worth of the horizons of significance. It is not a matter of whether they are or are not morally worthy, but a question of how we sift the good from the ugly or bad within the ones relevant to us. The horizons of significance are to be considered varied and ambiguous, and this puts back into the frame Taylor's emphatic proposal for dialogic rapport as a progressive method to advance authenticity. Notably, Taylor develops this in the same section as he introduces the horizons. Linked to the dialogic theme, a great deal also rests on the procedures and interactions being 'enframed by an ethic of caring' (p. 106), with the implicit appeal to the 'moral instincts' humans are said to possess, linked to 'our ineradicable sense that human life is to be respected.'[1] In terms of specifics, these are the main themes we have to use as we delve back into the various ideas that Taylor expresses.

Taylor's ineradicable view is that we cannot make an authentic moral choice based on pure pleasure, on immediate personal or interpersonal interests, or through any form of relativistic decision-making. As he conceives it, authenticity is not just about having freedom of choice; it is about choices made through an alliance with the template

---

[1] *Sources* p. 8.

and structure of 'horizons of significance'. But it is not by these alone: Taylor adds something that he elaborates in *Sources*, that rather lurks beneath the surface in *Authenticity*.[1] This is something we encountered early in our study, his sense, arising from the 'moral reactions' that come with being human, of 'a given ontology of the human'.[2]

This proposal of a 'moral ontology' arises from Taylor's conviction that deep moral instincts common in human experience count and matter.[3] He suggests that 'perhaps the most urgent and powerful cluster of demands that we recognize as moral concern the respect for life, integrity and well-being, even flourishing, of others'.[4] In historical and contemporary settings, Taylor thinks that these matters of concern count because, in situations of animosity and conflict, they are what we always most emphatically 'infringe.'

In *Authenticity*, Taylor puts a slightly more contemporary spin on the demands for an authentic life. He mentions the importance of 'fairness, which demands equal chances for everyone to develop their own identity' (p. 50); then there is 'in the intimate sphere, the identity-forming love relationship which has crucial importance'. The issue is how these modes of being can fit within the affiliated life of authenticity.

Central to this is an elevation in the notion of equality so that there is recognition, as within the plurality of modernity, of the right sense of 'the equal value of different ways of being' (p. 51). This form of equality has to do with how choices are made over matters of value. This means that 'just the fact that people *choose* different ways of being

---

[1] See for example *Authenticity* pp. 51-52
[2] *Sources* p. 5.
[3] *Sources* p. 8.
[4] *Sources* p. 4.

doesn't make them equal'. Equality, in the ontology of the human, comes in as we are, Taylor thinks, able to identify 'some properties, common or complimentary, which are of value'. These override the differences between distinct individuals and are what comes through the human capacity for 'reason, or love, or memory, or dialogical recognition'. These capacities enable agreement and the means to understand equality in the richer sense, and the outcome is that 'recognizing difference, like self-choosing, requires a horizon of significance, in this case a shared one' (p. 52).

Clearly, the many references in Taylor's text to disengaged rationality suggests that the capacity to think critically and positively has a key role, and Taylor equally clearly thinks that some aspects of the tradition are more important than others, namely, those with an organic, enmeshing and dialogic capacity. He affirms the 'practices' (p. 23) that conform to the ideals of authenticity, and the consistent implication is that so long as the right background ideas are used as a guide, the individual's search for authenticity will be justified, and the 'manner' and 'matter' (pp. 81-82) tension will be well sustained. In our conclusion, we will see a little more that Taylor adds to this mix.

The Problem of Authenticity as 'answerable to reason.'

In the second section of the book, Taylor makes three claims; that 'authenticity is a valid idea'; 'that you can argue in reason about ideals and about the conformity of practices to these ideals'; 'that these arguments can make a difference.' (pp. 22-23)

The key claim here is the ideal (authenticity – the ideal of being true to one's own identity), and the practices that conform to them are justifiable or answerable through 'reason', by which Taylor means 'reasoning' with particular reference to the detached objectivity of thought, 'disengaged rationality' (p. 25) as he terms it, that comes from Descartes.

Taylor develops this view in contrast with the attack he launches on subjectivism and relativism – neither of which can, he thinks, employ reason in a compelling manner. Taylor's view is that the ideal of authenticity implies practices – ways of living – that reason can explain and justify, thus showing that the ideal deserves to be followed. It is also possible to use reason to ensure that practices conform to the ideal and to audit and challenge practices that fail to meet the conditions of the ideal. By this means, Taylor can, of course, assail the distorted forms of the ideal (subjectivism and relativism). Taylor links to this to the claim that rational discussion can positively change things.

These proposals raise some engaging problems. To begin with, historically informed thinking might suggest that all forms of reasoning are impregnated with the reasoner's assumptions and values from the cultural mindset in question. Philosophical writers like Feuerbach and Marx variously argue that ideas (reason) are determined by life, and Nietzsche, considering the relation between the discipline of history and life, wrote that 'we want to serve history only to the extent that history serves life.'[1] Taylor never wants to renege on the enmeshed view of how human life rightly operates. However, when he elaborates his confidence in reason, this comes through his use of the concept of 'disengaged rationality' traced to Descartes. He has to work on something of a knife-edge, in that he wants to use this Cartesian notion, while he also thinks that Descartes errs and strays from the ways of good intellectual sense by taking 'a fateful step' (p. 102) and supposed that 'we *are* essentially disengaged reason; we are pure mind'. This alienates mind from body, and insofar as the Cartesian influence is considerable, this step does much to bring about the distortion of the ideal of authenticity.

In developing his positive 'work of retrieval' (p. 23), Taylor

---

[1] Nietzsche (1997) 2: Forward.

is, as we have seen, critical of the limitations of both calculative and instrumental forms of reason (pp. 101-102); he then recovers a sense of disengaged reason linked to the 'moral ideal... of a self-responsible, self-controlling reason' (p. 103). This is the method that has the fusion of critical and expressive rationality that fits with the ontology of dialogic relations in a life that operates within the context of accepting that human identity is developed and defined 'in a horizon of important questions' (p. 40), and in a dynamic that 'requires recognition by others' (p. 45).

Taylor thinks this rationale for disengaged and expressive rationality fits with and reflects the condition of relational and dialogical authenticity. This gives his variant of the view that the moral texture of life provides a basis for ethical reflection, but Taylor does this without the veneer of procedural methodology favoured by most ethicists.[1] The reciprocal regard of interpersonal life is the assumed way to texture this as the authentic mode of the ethical ideal and linked to rationality, it enables the judgments that aim to render plausible the ethical ideal of authenticity. As with his ideas on authenticity, Taylor does not encapsulate this rationale for reasoning in the text in as clear and definite a way as he might, but this is the shape of the proposal he has, and it is in much greater evidence in his more extended writing in *Sources of the Self*.[2]

Taylor and Democracy

In his last section, Taylor argues strongly for a mode of democratic action: 'the only effective counter to the drift towards atomism and instrumentalism built into market and bureaucratic state is the formation of an effective common purpose through democratic action, fragmentation disables us from resisting this drift. To lose the capacity to build politically effective majorities is to lose your paddle in mid-

---

[1] See the Introduction above.
[2] See *Sources* pp. 143-158 and pp. 321-354.

river' (pp. 117-118). This passage puts focus on a key problem within the malaises of modernity – 'atomism and instrumentalism' – and on 'democratic action', something that Taylor puts considerable emphasis hope on as the redemptive means by which the moral ideal of authenticity can come to expression.

Taylor claims, as in the opening section of his book, that the malaises of modernity, subjective individualism, instrumental reason and the loss of freedom have a net outcome of fragmenting and atomising humans to the detriment of associative forms of life. Humans thus tend to live in an isolated manner, becoming dysfunctional through an over-reliance on technologies. The danger that Taylor sees is arguably one that, some thirty years on, is even more explicit with the advent of smartphones and the plethora of social media platforms. In a hi-tech society, the problem of dependence is now well-known, with the level of dependence being likened to that of an addiction. 'Nomophobia' is the term in use to denote the fear of being without one's mobile phone and all the things that it brings.[1] Taylor's whole take on instrumentalism, fragmentation and atomism is built on the dangers that come with an increased dependence on and limitation by technology un-enframed by benevolent care.

While there are clear and present dangers to the commitments that some make to their smartphones and other instrumental technologies, there is a sense in which Taylor's objection feels like a polemic, an argument against the worst possible case. There is, in the face of this, some merit in considering a more balanced view. Taylor's 'worry' about technological abuses can be seen as something of a neurosis. Everything can be taken to an extreme to the point of distortion, whether we are dealing with technologies or turnips. Of course, there is the threat

---

[1] Here one can consult the online guide: Smartphone Addiction – Helpguide.org

of over-dependence on mobile devices. However, a core reason for the significance that mobile phones and associated devices have is that they serve as mediums for communicative, associative relations. Arguably, in and for a pluralistic age of considerable social mobility, the communicative platforms accessed through mobile devices do much good for 'dialogic' life.[1]

Taylor's common argument is of avoiding extremes of knocking or boosting over the trends he examines, and in the case of the problems of fragmentation against democratic participation, it is worth pointing out that it is well-known that, particularly in the campaigns for the American presidential elections since 2008, and in the parliamentary campaigns run for the UK elections from 2010 to 2019, smart technology and the social media played a considerable part in engaging prospective voters in the democratic process.

Despite this, within mature democracies, levels of participation in elections are of increasing concern. The Brexit referendum in the UK in 2016 led to a victory for the Leave campaign by 52% to 48%. However, the vote involved 72% of the electorate, so the winning 52% of votes were cast by 37% of the electorate: this means that 35% of the electorate voted against and a further 28% did not vote. In one sense, this is how it was, and it is not our concern to reflect on how and why people decided to act to give these results. What is of greater importance is that in media terms, all that was in the air was that '52%' had voted to leave, with the implication that this was a distinct majority. Of course, it was nothing like a clear majority in real terms, which is a partial explanation for why polarised and incommensurable Brexit debates clogged up the UK parliament – a representative and deliberative assembly – for the next three years.

---

[1] Even more so in the time of Covid restrictions.

The emergent view that matters here is that the majority of elections are like this, with less-than-optimal voter turn-out and majorities achieved on less than a majority of the popular vote. In large part, this is due to the way in which intelligent social market research enables parties to focus the message to target the crucial floating voters in specific constituencies. As in the UK election of 2019, the Conservatives achieved a comprehensive landslide victory, demolishing the so-called 'red wall' of Labour strongholds in the former industrial heartlands to gain an 80-seat majority in parliament with a vote share of 43.6%. Even the 2020 US Presidential election, which was widely reported to have had the highest number of votes cast in such elections, voter turn-out was 66.9%.[1]

Dangers arise from this: those who are elected are decreasingly representative of the total electorate and so become more likely of seeming and perhaps of being detached or despotic. Underlying this are the dangers Taylor notes of atomisation and fragmentation. People lose the capacity to form a common purpose and carry it out: fragmentation arises when people come to be more and more atomistic, living in increasing self-regarding isolation, as the bonds and common interests with their fellow citizens deteriorate. A fragmented society is one whose members find it harder and harder to identify their political society with a community. Taylor thinks that this fragmentation comes about partly through a weakening of the bonds of sympathy, partly in a self-feeding way, and through the democratic initiative's failure. As set out in the final section of *Authenticity*, his alternative is to promote a rescaled and downsized localised activism set up on clearly democratic lines, to recharge an engaged, socially committed style of reform and development.

Taylor's thinking on democracy and its discontents received

_____

[1] Figures from. economictimes.com

an update in 2016 when Joshua Rothman reported on his visit to the Social Science Research Council in New York for *The New Yorker* magazine.[1]

Taylor was involved in a public seminar with graduate students, and Rothman gives some clear pointers to the ideas that Taylor had under the heading 'How to Restore Your Faith in Democracy.' The seminar came a fortnight or so after Donald Trump had rather unexpectedly beaten Hillary Clinton to become, at that stage President-Elect.

Taylor was in no way pleased by this outcome, but his point about it was analytically astute. One major strand in the ideal of democracy is that it 'is supposed to be a system in which non-élites have a say.'[2] Whatever else Trump was about, he had achieved something that defended this aspect of democracy.

Taylor commented on how he has sensed since childhood something he had later studied, which was that in the 1930s, in Canada and the USA, there had been a clear sense that political certainty was dangerous. This was due to the awareness that was growing of National Socialism in Germany and Soviet Communism under Stalin in Russia. In reaction, the prevailing view in North America was to periodically elect a pragmatic specialist 'élite team.' This would avoid wild extremes and hold to a moderate centre-ground.

Given the progression of life and the changes in the patterns of activity that Taylor considers significant, it is no surprise that he comes to a different view. For the current climate, he favours a tradition that would include Aristotle,

[1] The New Yorker, 11/11/2016, available online @
www.newyorker.com/culture/persons-of-interest/
[2] Quotations are from the New Yorker, as per the previous footnote.

Machiavelli, Hannah Arendt, Rousseau and Montesquieu.[1] Here were thinkers who, despite their differences of time and emphasis, all thought that 'it's a higher mode of being to participate in your own self-government'.

Rothman notes that Taylor bases this sense of how we would best be, assuming that the sense of individual selfhood derives 'from shared values that are, in turn, embodied in public institutions'. Here 'public institutions' appear to be a localised version of horizons of significance. This leads to a version of developed democratic participation through the notion and policy of 'subsidiarity', a view defended by de Tocqueville and Catholicism, whereby 'problems should be solved by people who are nearby.' The implication is that localised democratic participation is non-ideological, and places the emphasis for political activity 'on local schools, town governments, voluntary associations, and churches.'

We have a strong echo of New England transcendentalism, with Rothman, who in his final comments, envisages:

'a house in the woods with the television turned off. Inside, family members aren't glued to their phones. They talk, over dinner, about politics, history, and faith, about national movements and local ones; they feel, all the time, that they are doing something. It's a pastoral vision, miles away from the media-driven election we've just concluded. But it's not fantasy.'

---

[1] Here is mention of thinkers, two of whom we have not yet encountered: Niccolò Machiavelli (1469-1527), Florentine diplomat, historian, and writer. Writings include *The Prince* (1513), a lucid work of political thought which suggests how in real life, for the sake of glory, power and wealth, anything goes. Hannah Arendt – as mentioned earlier in this text, was a refugee from Nazi Germany, and she was influential in the early years of developing the Social Science Research Council in New York. Charles-Louis de Secondat, Baron de Montesquieu (1689-1755). French lawyer and political thinker whose book *The Spirit of Law* (1748) developed a clear and influential theory on the separation of powers.

From Rothman's piece, Taylor's later ideas fit in pretty closely with the ideas he developed in the final section of *The Ethics of Authenticity*. Again we see that Taylor views the democratic situation as one that still gives a platform for the work of issues-based persuasion and retrieval that he encourages at the local level.

All-round, the analysis that Taylor gives in the 1991 and the 2016 vintages resonate with a more recent analysis of the predicament of modern democracy, as expressed in *Twilight of Democracy* (2020), by the historian and political commentator Anne Applebaum. In this book, she reflects on the emergent condition of the developed societies within which democracy is getting into the sorts of difficulty Taylor notices.

Applebaum thinks that the liberal democratic political state is now typically rich in pluralistic complexity.[1] This can be seen as a marvellous asset, but the problem is that many people find difficulty living with this complex modernity. Losing a sense of identity with the political class and system, people in more everyday situations look for something else. As with those who supported Trump in 2016 and 2020, they yearn for the simplicity of a singular narrative and are thus attracted to authoritarian ideals. They respond to figures who offer solutions that have specific aims and targets. In modernity, such campaigners can utilise social media platforms to 'bundle together issues, repackage them, and then market them'.[2] Campaigning in this way does not try to sell ideologies but to construct a frame of mind that will respond to a certain message in a specific way come the time for an election. 'Unity, harmony and tradition' are, Applebaum suggests, the themes that recur in such campaigns.[3] These themes have a strong

---

[1] See Applebaum (2020) p. 106.
[2] Applebaum (2020) p. 123.
[3] See Applebaum (2020) p. 124.

leaning towards, at best 'nostalgic', at worst, a more 'authoritarian' and essentially undemocratic outcome.[1]

A lesson we can take from Applebaum and Taylor as regards liberal democracy is that as a political system, it is devalued if it is not engaged in a deliberative and participatory way in and through localised ventures. Democracy is to be seen as a ground-up approach to the political settlement. Set against this as a clear and present danger is the risk is of the much-touted phenomenon of democracy resulting in an elected government with an over-specific, particularistic agenda. Such a government might have been elected by the people, but it will not be a government for all or even many people.

Taylor is alert to this issue and is especially keen to avoid distortions of all types. This is one reason why he wants to promote activism that has a focus on localised issues that have, he hopes, a better prospect of engaging more authentic support. This aspiration is linked to Taylor's pragmatic view of what he envisages as a continuing struggle in the project of retrieval.

---

[1] See Applebaum (2020) pp. 64-65 and p. 16.

13. Taylor's Project – Conclusions

Here we need to draw breath and appreciate something from the firmament of political history, which is that the relatively recent phenomenon of democratic liberalism harks back to the values and aspirations of the European Enlightenment. This was a period when human worth and dignity was centred on rationality and ethical personhood. It is less often recalled that Enlightenment thought, which tended not to regard humanity as fallen as in the sense of regressive theologies, nevertheless saw humans as finite, as incomplete, as in a state of transition and process. An implication is that humanity does not have the easy option of completion or fulfilment. A worry, linked to those Taylor identifies at the start of his book, is that too many in the most recent modernity assume that the human condition can rest on a uniform possibility of being rendered into a finished product, often manifest through the endearing assumption that each age or period, or worse, each aspect of the complex plurality, considers it has reached definitive insights into life as we know it.

All-round, there is an everyday form of realism inherent in Taylor's persuasive enterprise of retrieval in that he is in line with the Enlightenment view of human limitability; his ethical ideal of authenticity emerges through the text of *The Ethics of Authenticity* as a kind of tightrope act with the aim of persuasion in the face of an uncertain and ongoing struggle. His argument is on a high wire, and the safety net is at one remove in the depth and detail of *Sources of the Self*. In *Authenticity*, we have the affirmation of the individual being true to him or her-self; this condition of life is not seen as self-seeking, egoistic or privatised, although it does seem clear that the risks of these deviations remain. The ideal of authenticity is conceived as dialogic, empowered by disengaged rationality and self-responsible freedom, and girded by the discerned positive principles emitted by the horizons of society, culture, history, nature, and, perhaps, deeper metaphysical and theological perspectives. In *Authenticity*, these are affirmed with explanatory validation, mostly through a narrative in which the pieces, like characters in a story, are eventually assembled into a family gathering, and where appeal to the principle of respect for persons and life has to bear considerable weight.[1]

Taylor puts a special value on traditions that have the scope of a narrative past, and the concern he works to sketch and resolve in *Authenticity* is, as we know, built on the larger project of *Sources*, where he sought to retrieve 'buried goods'.[2] The 'goods' interred here were not commodities, but abiding values, and the burial he has in mind is due to several earth-moving influences: a form of 'modern naturalism', modes of 'partisan narrowness', 'the terrible experiences of millenarian destructiveness', and 'layers of philosophical rationale'. These combine to 'read so many goods out of our story'. Accordingly, in *Sources*, even more than in *Authenticity*, Taylor is engaged in a form of excavation to unearth and represent the authentic form of being human. What 'being true to oneself' (p. 15) is all about is a layered way of being in relationship, it entails the possibility of an active, engaged mode of life within a wider social plurality, giving the sense of individuality being varied and variable within dialogic parameters, operating with reference to rational capacity and inescapable horizons, and held together by the appeal to mutual respect, and, in *Sources*, with an appeals to the Christian notion of *agapē,* and to what Taylor terms 'constitutive' goods.[3]

The tension that can be seen with the solution that Taylor presents in *Authenticity* remains that, in the text, we receive a perspective of an ethical outlook with the ideal of authenticity proposing an operational stance for how we

---

[1] See *Sources* p. 8 and Chapter 1 above.
[2] *Sources* p. 520.
[3] See *Sources* pp. 513-517 and pp. 92-93.

should be as active agents within the political, social, and cultural dimensions of life. There is a deliberate avoidance of providing a normative guide to the business of doing life as self-determining individuals day-to-day. In this, we find both the strength and the limitation of Taylor's ethic of authenticity. If the hope is for a more distinct and ordered arrangement of ideas to give Taylor's proposals a more compelling shape, we have to work back through the larger enterprise of *Sources* to consider the 'package' there unwrapped.[1]

For any reader of *Authenticity*, the pattern of ideas in the earlier and much more extensive work will seem familiar. Taylor defends the socio-cultural scenario with plural or multiple notions of the good, a 'diversity of goods, for which a valid claim can be made.'[2] An example is that 'the dignity that attaches to disengaged reason is not invalidated when we see how expressive fulfilment or ecological responsibility has been savaged in its name.' As Taylor sees it, historical philosophising shows both the extent of the savagery here, and the abiding worth of disengaged rationality. This mode of reasoning expresses a sense of fulfilment and responsibility over the wider environment and is embedded in what it is to be authentically human. All of this is encompassed in the sense of the ideal of authenticity, where life is conceived as relational or dialogic and so as embodying ethical principles.

What Taylor is consistent in opposing are perspectives that have a singular and narrow proposal. The outcome is that such approaches 'find their way through the dilemmas of modernity by invalidating some of the crucial goods in contest.'[3] In his writings, Taylor consistently opposes the view that human life operates on some narrow and exclusive platform, whether it is of nationalism, emotive feeling,

---

[1] See *Sources* p. 503.
[2] *Sources* p. 502.
[3] *Sources* p. 503.

241

passionate self-expression, or calculative utility. The diverse goods proposed in *Sources of the Self* are, in contrast, inclusive:

'a sense of self defined by the powers of disengaged reason as well as of the creative imagination, in the characteristically modern understandings of freedom and dignity and rights, in the ideals of self-fulfilment and expression, and in the demands of universal benevolence and justice.'

Taylor puts enormous weight on the way that, from a practical, everyday point of view, we simply cannot work effectively with these modern, aspirational values unless we also have 'recourse to these strongly valued goods for the purposes of life: deliberating, judging situations, deciding how you feel about people, and the like.'[1] It is this dialogic reality that underpins his rejection of the metaethical projects in modern philosophy.[2]

To see how Taylor links the moral sources that matter to modernity's challenges, we need to look more at his defence of what we mentioned above, his idea of a 'constitutive good.'[3] This notion comes through a review Taylor makes on how it will be possible to articulate a sense of 'the good as a moral source' to give it 'power'. Taylor is clear that seeing the good in this sense is something that has 'been deeply suppressed in the mainstream of modern moral consciousness, although it was perfectly familiar to the ancients'. This shows Taylor's ongoing allegiance to his views on certain more arid forms of philosophical reflection, as from his time as a student at Oxford. We might also recall the thought from early in our study of *Authenticity* that Taylor seemed to hint at something of an

---

[1] *Sources* p. 59.
[2] See *Sources* Part 1.
[3] *Sources* p. 92.

affinity with Platonic notions of the good.[1] In *Sources*, this hint relates to some weighty fruit, in that the development of moral sources undertaken is related to Platonic thought, in part, through an affinity Taylor notes with Murdoch's thinking as expressed in, for example, her study *The Sovereignty of Good* (1970).[2]

Murdoch's approach, also expressed in her novels, was that in modernity, especially in the mid-twentieth century, there was abundant evidence of what happened if human value systems were elevated as absolute truth. There were the extremes of, on one side, the chaos, devastation and myriad tyrannies from totalitarian regimes, and on the other, a fall towards a directionless kind of relativism where passions overwhelmed any sense of reason or the good.[3] The problem in modernity is that human thought has eradicated the 'values' previously given some form of eternal status. Instead, 'the idea of the good remains indefinable and empty so that human choice may fill it'.[4] Here Murdoch gives a crisp anticipatory summary of Taylor's later enterprise against the 'knockers'.

Murdoch's remedy was a revisionist look at Platonic ideas, particularly the idea of the Good. She comments that 'as an ethical system cannot but commend an ideal, it should commend a worthy ideal'.[5] A thought not lost on Taylor, it seems. What Murdoch suggests is we should think of the Good as 'a perfection which is perhaps never exemplified in the world we know… and which carries with it the ideas of hierarchy and transcendence'.[6] We know that 'the very great are not the perfect' because 'we see differences, we

---

[1] See Chapter 2 above and Plato (2007) 517c and 519c.
[2] See Sources pp. 95-93 and n. 4 especially.
[3] Two of Murdoch's novels that are relevant here are *The Bell* (1958) and *The Good Apprentice* (1985). See Murdoch (2019) and (2000).
[4] Murdoch (1970) p. 80.
[5] Murdoch (1970) p. 78.
[6] Murdoch (1970) p. 93.

sense directions, and we know that the Good is still somewhere beyond':

'The self, the place where we live, is a place of illusion. Goodness is connected with the attempt to see the unself, to see and respond to the real world in the light of a virtuous consciousness. This is the non-metaphysical meaning of transcendence to which philosophers have so constantly resorted in their explanations of goodness. "Good is a transcendent reality" means that virtue is the attempt to pierce the veil of selfish consciousness and join the world as it really is. It is an empirical fact about human nature that this attempt cannot be entirely successful'.

The outcome of this for Murdoch is that the Good, while 'non-representable and indefinable', is nevertheless, indeed, because of this, 'as a transcendent magnetic centre… the least corruptible and most realistic picture for us to use in our reflections on the moral life'.[1]

These thoughts influence Taylor, and in *Sources*, he looks to develop a recovered sense of 'the good' with, akin to Murdoch, a sense of hierarchy, that he terms 'rational order'.[2] Coupled with the rational sense is the ability to 'love this order', which entails seeing how our actions and motivations tie into 'a cosmic reality, the order of things'. This suggestion calls to mind Taylor's view in *Authenticity* that human identity can only be realised 'against the background of things that matter' (p. 40). What we find in *Sources* is that what really matters as the background is the 'reality' of the relationship between our 'action and motivation' and 'the Idea of the good itself'.[3] It is the relation here that 'makes certain of our actions or aspirations good'. It is a Platonic principle that Taylor reaffirms that suggests that the goods we are thus linked to are 'modes of life'.[4] It follows that these goods 'are facets

---

[1] Murdoch (1970) p. 74 and p. 75.
[2] *Sources* p. 92.
[3] *Sources* p. 92.
[4] *Sources* p. 93

244

or components of a good life' and that they can be termed 'life goods'. Taylor moves to say that the 'life goods refer us to some features of the way things are, in virtue of which these life goods are goods. This feature constitutes them as goods', and so Taylor calls them 'constitutive':

'The constitutive good does more than just define the content of the moral theory. Love of it is what empowers us to be good. And hence also loving it is part of what it is to be a good human being. This is now part of the content of the moral theory as well, which includes injunctions not only to act in certain ways and to exhibit certain moral qualities but also to love what is good'.

Rational agency is intimately connected to Taylor's sense of this moral source and to the human capacity to have the courage to disengage with the 'disenchanted universe' of modernity.[1] However, the theme of *La Lotta Continua* is something of a presence here, in that Taylor remains of the view that 'in the climate of modern moral philosophy' there has been a general 'eclipse of our whole awareness of qualitative distinction' that an appreciation of constitutive goods requires. The battle is to overcome 'the neglect of this whole dimension of our moral thought and experience'.[2]

If we return to *The Ethics of Authenticity,* we can better appreciate how it outlines the positive pluralism of diverse goods and the moral source and real moral ideal that Taylor gives fuller attention to in *Sources. Authenticity* is rounded off with a call to action, to life and to the challenges that are commensurate with the ongoing dynamic of life, to work on what Taylor terms:

'...a complex and many-levelled struggle, intellectual, spiritual, and political, in which the debates in the public arena interlink with those in a host of individual settings, like hospitals and schools, where the issues of enframing technology are being lived through in concrete form; and where these disputes in turn both

---

[1] *Sources* p. 94.
[2] *Sources* p. 95.

feed and are fed by the various attempts to define in theoretical terms the place of technology and the demands of authenticity, and beyond that, the shape of human life and its place in the cosmos' (p. 120).

Life in a Covid-alert age was not in Taylor's mind when he wrote this, but the focus and orientation of his remarks are rather apposite to this emergent phase of life for humanity.

This points to the view that in the time since Taylor published *The Ethics of Authenticity*, nothing that has happened suggests that he was wrong to think that life will continue to engage in ongoing and layered struggles over the tensions between the personal and extra-personal aspects of being human. Struggles over whether, how, and in what form to define and develop authentic forms for human life will undoubtedly continue for finite and largely imperfectible humanity. Taylor's insistence on the merits of 'inescapable horizons' should be seen as the most powerful and most controversial support for the commitment he has to authenticity, linked to fusing self-determination with dialogic relations. Sometimes a thinker has a job to avoid being seen as trying to square the circle: we mentioned this with Taylor earlier, but with the attempt to hold authenticity together with the horizons of significance, adding self-determination as well as dialogic relations to the bundle, and seeing this as all related to the defence of the moral ideal of the Good as the constitutive source for value, his complex task has been more to convince us that these perspectives can be held together in a persuasive harmony.

Bibliography

Abbey, R. (2004) – Editor – *Charles Taylor*. Cambridge: Cambridge University Press.

Antonaccio, M and Sweiker, W. (1996) *Iris Murdoch and the Search for Human Goodness*. Chicago: University of Chicago Press.

Applebaum, A. (2020) *Twilight of Democracy.* New York: Doubleday.

Arendt, H. (1959) *The Human Condition*. Garden City NJ: Doubleday.

Berlin, I. (2017) *Liberty*. Edited by Henry Hardy, with an essay on 'Berlin and his Critics' by Ian Harris. Oxford, Oxford University Press.

Bloom, A. (1987) *The Closing of the American Mind*. New York: Simon and Schuster.

Borgman, A. (1984) *Technology and the Character of Contemporary Life*. Menlo Park, CA: Addison-Wesley.

Buber, M. (2000) *I and Thou.* Translated by R. Gregor-Smith. New York: Scribners.

Burleigh, M. (2000) *The Third Reich: A New History*. London: Macmillan.

Cantwell-Smith, W. (1978) *The Meaning and End of Religion.* New York: Harper Row.

Donne, J. (1959) *Devotions Upon Emergent Occasions*. Michigan: University of Michigan Press/Ann Arbor Paperbacks.

Eliade, M. (1959) *The Sacred and the Profane*. Translated by W R Trask. New York: Harcourt, Brace and World.

Foot, Philippa.(2003) *Natural Goodness*. Oxford: Oxford University Press.

247

Hardy, H. (2018) *In Search of Isaiah Berlin*. London: I.B. Taurus.

Hatab, L. (2000) *Ethics and Finitude*. Lanham, Rowman & Littlefield.

Heidegger, Martin. (2001) *Being and Time*. Translated by J Macquarrie and E. Robinson, Oxford: Blackwells.

Herder, J. G. von (2002) *Philosophical Writings*. Translated and Edited by M. N. Forster, Cambridge: Cambridge University Press.

Ignatieff, M. (2001) *The Needs of Strangers*. London: Picador.

Joyce, H. (2021) *TRANS When Ideology Meets Reality*. London, ONEWORLD.

Kant, I. (2019) *Groundwork of the Metaphysic of Morals*. Translated and introduced by C Bennett, J Saunders and R Stern. Oxford: Oxford World's Classics.

Kerr, F. (2004) 'The Self and the Good: Taylor's Moral Ontology' in Abbey (2004) pp. 84-104.

Lasch, C. (2018) *The Culture of Narcissism*. Introduced by E. J. Dionne Jr. New York & London: W. W. Norton.

Lasch, C. (1984) *The Minimal Self*. New York & London: W. W. Norton.

Loxton, S. (2020) *Words and Deeds: An Introduction to the Thought of Ludwig Wittgenstein*. (Revised Second Edition) London: New Generation Press.

Loxton, S. (2021) *Nietzsche and the Old Flame. An Introduction and Guide to Nietzsche and On the Genealogy of Morals*. London: New Generation Press.

MacIntyre, A. (1981) *After Virtue*. London: Duckworth.

Macquarrie, J. (1982) *In Search of Humanity*. London: SCM.

Marx, K and Engels, F. (2015) *The Communist Manifesto*. London: Penguin.

Mead, G. H. (1934) *Mind, Self and Society*. Chicago: Chicago University Press.

Mill, J. S. (1967) *A System of Logic*. London: Longmans.

Mill, J. S. (1987) *On Liberty*. Introduction by Gertrude Himmelfarb. Harmondsworth: Penguin Classics.

Miller, D. (Editor) (2006) *The Liberty Reader*. New York: Routledge.

Montaigne, Michel De (2003). *The Complete Essays*. Translated and edited with an Introduction and Notes by M. A. Screech. London: Penguin.

Murdoch, I. (1970) *The Sovereignty of Good*. London: Routledge and Kegan Paul.

Murdoch, I. (2000) *The Good Apprentice*. Introduced by D.E. Cooper. London: Vintage Classics.

Murdoch, I. (2003) *Metaphysics as a Guide to Morals*. London: Vintage Classics.

Murdoch, I. (2019) *The Bell*. Introduced by S. Perry. London: Vintage Classics.

Nietzsche, F. (1974) *The Gay Science*. Translated, with a commentary by W. Kaufmann. New York: Vintage.

Nietzsche, F. (1998*) Beyond Good and Evil*. Translated and edited M. Faber. Introduction by R. C. Holub. Oxford World Classics: Oxford.

Nietzsche, F. (2008) *On the Genealogy of Morals*. Translated, with introduction and notes, by D. Smith. Oxford World Classics: Oxford.

Nietzsche, F. (1997) *Untimely Meditations*. Edited by D. Breazeale. Translated by R. J. Hollingdale. Cambridge University Press: Cambridge.

Otto, R. (1958) *The Idea of the Holy*. Translated by J. W. Harvey. Oxford: Oxford University Press.

Plato (2007) *The Republic*. (Translated by D. Lee with an Introduction by M. Lane). London: Penguin Classics.

Pope, A. (2011) *The Rape of the Lock and Other Major Writings*. Introduction by L. Damrash. London: Penguin Classics.

Sartre, J-P. (1980) *Existentialism and Humanism*. Translated P. Mairet. London: Methuen.

Shakespeare, W. (2012) *The Tempest*. London: Collins.

Sheehy, G. (1976) *Passages: Predictable Crises of Adult Life*. New York: Bantam Books.

Shelley, P. B. (2017) *Selected Poems*. Edited by J. Donavan and C. Duffy. London: Penguin Classics.

Schiller, F.C.F. (1967) *On the Aesthetic Education of Man*. Translated by E. Wilkinson and L. A. Willoughby. Oxford: The Clarendon Press.

Schumacher, E. F. (1974) *Small is Beautiful: A Study of Economics as if People Really Mattered*. London: Sphere.

Shakespeare, W. (2016) *King Henry IV Part 2*. Edited by J. C. Bulman. London and New York: Bloomsbury.

Singer, P. (2011) *Practical Ethics* (Third Edition). Cambridge: Cambridge University Press.

Smart, N. (1971) *The Religious Experience of Mankind*. London: Fontana.

Taylor, C. (1975) *Hegel*. Cambridge: Cambridge University Press.

Taylor, C. (1979) *Hegel and Modern Society*. Cambridge: Cambridge University Press.

Taylor, C. (1991) *The Malaise of Modernity*. Toronto: Anansi.

Taylor, C. (1996) 'Iris Murdoch and Moral Philosophy' in Antonaccio, M and Sweiker, W. (1996) *Iris Murdoch and the Search for Human Goodness*. Chicago: University of Chicago Press (pp. 3-28). The essay is also pp. 2-23 in Taylor (2014) below.

Taylor, C. (2003) *The Ethics of Authenticity*. Cambridge MA: Harvard University Press.

Taylor, C. (2004) *Modern Social Imaginaries*. Durham and London: Duke University Press.

Taylor, C. (2006) 'What's Wrong With Negative Liberty?' in Miller, D. (Editor) *The Liberty Reader*. New York: Routledge.

Taylor, C. (2007) *A Secular Age*. Cambridge MA: Harvard University Press.

Taylor, C. (2010) *Sources of the Self: The Making of the Modern Identity*. Cambridge: Cambridge University Press.

Taylor, C. (2014) *Dilemmas and Connections. Selected Essays*. Cambridge MA: Belnap/Harvard University Press.

Taylor, C. (2014) 'Conditions of an Unforced Consensus on Human Rights', in *Dilemmas and Connections. Selected Essays*. Cambridge MA: Belnap/Harvard University Press (pp. 105-123).

Taylor, C. (2014) 'Notes on the Sources of Violence: Perennial and Modern', in *Dilemmas and Connections. Selected Essays*. Cambridge MA: Belnap/Harvard University Press (pp 188-213).

Taylor, C. (2014) 'Disenchantment – Reenchantment', in *Dilemmas and Connections. Selected Essays*. Cambridge MA: Belnap/Harvard University Press (pp 287-302).

Taylor, C. (2014) 'Perils of Moralism', in *Dilemmas and Connections. Selected Essays*. Cambridge MA: Belnap/Harvard University Press (pp. 347-366).

Trilling, L. (1972) *Sincerity and Authenticity*. Cambridge, MA: Harvard University Press.

Wasserman, E. (1968) *The Subtler Language*. Baltimore: John Hopkins University Press.

Weber, M. (2005) *The Protestant Ethic and the Spirit of Capitalism*. Translated by T. Parsons. London and New York: Routledge.

Wordsworth, W. (1995) *The Prelude. The Four Texts* (1798, 1799, 1805, 1850). Edited by J. Wordsworth. London, Penguin Classics.

Acknowledgements

As noted at the outset, this book originates in a study guide written for I.B. Philosophy students at Sherborne School for Girls. I am grateful for the stimulus the generations of students gave in the years we gave our minds to Taylor and his thoughts on authenticity.

Work on the book was started in Zambia in 2020 during the first wave of Covid19. More work was done during self-isolation when I was in the UK for a family wedding in October 2020. Back in Zambia, I worked on completing the first draft in the early part of 2021. Other projects then took precedence, but I was able to finish and revise the book later in the year.

I am most grateful to Dr Henry Hardy of Wolfson College, Oxford, for his generous help in aiding me in deliberations over the provenance of Taylor's 'horizons of significance', and even more to Professor Charles Taylor for clarifying that his thinking on these matters comes from his interest in the phenomenological school of thought, especially the work of Merleau-Ponty.

My thanks to my family and friends for their support and understanding, and thanks again to Hilda Chintu, Manager of 6lightmedia of East Park, Lusaka, for the efficient production of photocopies of the final drafts of the text, a great help in checking and proofreading. Abigail Mumbi has also given much-appreciated help and support in the final period of work on this book, not least with help on picture research.

As ever, my thanks to the team at New Generation Publishing for their care over the production of the book.

Finally, referring to the dedication at the start of this book, this is for my good friend Mark Felstead. He deserves this dedication for his support, commitment, and defence of academic and collegiate values within the professional life we shared as Heads of Department at Sherborne School for Girls and his continued support and friendship.

Stephen Loxton

Index

258

T

U

V

W

Printed in Great Britain
by Amazon